PRAISE FOR
THE EVERYDAY ADVOCATE

The Everyday Advocate is illuminating. It breaks the mold for what we expect Christian advocacy to look like and comes at a critical time for the progressive movement. Murray translates his depth of knowledge into a tactical field guide that anyone can use to level up their advocacy. He expertly weaves together personal experience and others' success stories to light a path forward for novices and career activists alike.

—Brian Derrick, political strategist and founder of Oath Advising

Ross Murray epitomizes finding your calling in life and using it. His work for the LGBTQ community has led to change that has saved lives and opened hearts and minds. It is a privilege to work with him every day and see him live his passion.

—Sarah Kate Ellis, president and CEO, GLAAD

In a world in which we can often feel powerless, Ross writes an inspiring book about ways we can make a difference. His personal stories and positive writing style make his suggestions and guidance accessible and encouraging. I especially appreciated the honest, genuine faith perspective Ross brings to this work, which will make it especially useful in congregations and communities. In this book, Ross shares meaningful, transformational opportunities to deepen our impact and discipleship. I highly recommend *The Everyday Advocate*.

—Bishop Paul Egensteiner, Metropolitan New York Synod, Evangelical Lutheran Church in America

How can someone best advocate for LGBTQ people in their daily life? That's a challenging question for many people. To make it even more challenging, we could ask: How can someone

advocate for LGBTQ people in their daily life and draw from their own religious beliefs to do so? For an increasing number of believers, that is not only a challenging question but an essential one. Ross Murray's new book provides a smart, inviting, accessible, hopeful, and faith-filled roadmap for answering both of these questions, reminding us that the liberation of all people is at the heart of the Gospels.

—Rev. James Martin, SJ, editor at large, America Media

I'm excited for Ross Murray's book *The Everyday Advocate* because it may be the catalyst that turns a voter into a lifelong activist who organizes their friends, family, neighborhood, town, county, region, state, or country to reach its fullest potential. The possibilities are endless once one realizes they have power to build and wield.

—Sarah Reeske, organizing manager, Invisible–New York State; co-leader, Indivisible, Mohawk Valley, Clinton, NY

Ross Murray has poured a lifetime of faith-inspired justice experience into this handbook for new and seasoned advocates. He offers practical guidance that demystifies advocacy and promotes it as an expression of Christian vocation that includes strategies, insights, and action steps. His personal stories of growth as a Christian and as an advocate invite others to take the first step or to deepen their practice. Ross emphasizes the relational nature of advocacy, encouraging the reader to connect to communities of suffering and join communities of action to inform and drive their public witness.

—Rev. Amy Reumann, senior director for Witness in Society, Evangelical Lutheran Church in America

THE EVERYDAY
ADVOCATE

The
EVERYDAY
ADVOCATE

Living Out
Your Calling
to Social Justice

Ross Murray

Fortress Press

Minneapolis

THE EVERYDAY ADVOCATE
Living Out Your Calling to Social Justice

Cover design and illustration: Brad Norr Design

Print ISBN: 978-1-5064-8543-0
eBook ISBN: 978-1-5064-8544-7

This book is dedicated to everyday advocates, wherever they are. Parents who are holding their school board accountable for quality education. Families initiating difficult but necessary conversations with their neighbors that put news of climate devastation and racism into context. The constituents who are in constant contact with their elected leaders, urging them to work for justice.

This book is for everybody who hears the news, shakes their head, says a little prayer, and then figures out what they can do to make our world a little better.

CONTENTS

CONTENTS

ACKNOWLEDGMENTS

I approached this book with a little trepidation, knowing that I had my own experiences and learnings to share but also aware of how many different ways people are working to change the world for the better.

There are so many advocates—working in their own spaces, doing such incredible work. In this book, I attempt to shine a spotlight on a handful of people who have taught me how to envision a better world and strategically work toward it. You'll hear the stories of some of my colleagues and friends, including Emily Eastwood, DaShawn Usher, and Conie Borchardt. You'll also hear about the people and organizations that are making a difference, even if I haven't yet met the leaders, like Rev. William Barber, Leah Greenberg, and Ezra Levin. There are advocates working in all corners of the world, and I tried to include bits of their wisdom in these pages.

I am thankful for the organizations that I've worked for and partnered with. They have informed the wisdom I will be sharing with you. My colleagues at GLAAD have thick skins, recognizing the world as it is and advocating for a world with 100 percent acceptance of the LGBTQ community. The staff and volunteers at ReconcilingWorks are a scrappy bunch who organized to change one of the largest churches in America for the better. Local communities like Indivisible Harlem and Empire State Indivisible provided my husband, Richard, and I with community and encouragement and made the confusing tangle of New York City and State politics much more accessible. Programs like Vote Forward gave us something tangible to do during election cycles that seemed bleak. We found ways to keep working on the issues that mattered to us, and I hope this book can help you find something you can do to address injustice and make this world a little better.

I deeply appreciate Fortress Press for giving me a platform to share what I've learned and apply it to people's lives in a tangible way. Beth Gaede brought me into the Fortress Press family and encouraged my writing as a way to share my learnings with others who want to act but just don't know what to do. Laura Gifford's editing, comments, and questions helped shape this book into something tangible and useful.

The mentality of justice has to be instilled and nurtured, and I'm grateful to have a family that encourages fairness, helpfulness, inclusion, and acceptance. All my immediate family members work in education, opening up minds to the wide possibility of the world and encouraging people to be their best selves. Even as the one who didn't go into education, I find myself still in a role of teaching others, and I'm grateful for their support and influence.

A final word of thank-you to my husband, Richard Garnett. When we were first dating, we had a profound conversation about altruism and selfishness. Richard asked if someone could be truly altruistic or if there was always something people were getting back for themselves. I've carried that conversation with me through our relationship as well as my advocacy work. Over the years, Richard supported my jobs at advocacy nonprofits while he did corporate work. Did he do it out of pure altruism? We'll never know! Richard left his corporate career to turn to advocacy in an effort to make this world better. While I'm working my job at GLAAD or doing any of a hundred side projects, he attends Indivisible meetings and DemCast briefings, organizes visits with our elected leaders, and canvasses and makes phone calls for the candidates we believe in. Richard is dedicating himself to electing leaders who will tax fairly, reduce income inequality, combat climate change, and ensure health care and affordable housing for all, among other things. He's also a contributor to this book, sharing his own stories, providing examples, and bringing his passion for becoming an everyday advocate. We are closer as a couple, sometimes working together and sometimes doing parallel work. But the partnership remains strong.

Finally, I give thanks to you, dear reader. You are already doing so much to keep communities stable and advance justice in big and small ways. Some days, you will give 10 percent, others 100 percent. There will be times when giving 1 percent will be a challenge. We need you in this movement now and in the long haul doing whatever you can. I am grateful for your partnership in this work.

INTRODUCTION

When I was fourteen years old, I was confirmed at a little church in northern Minnesota where my family were members. After two years of Wednesday-night confirmation instruction, including memorization of the Lord's Prayer, Apostles' Creed, and Ten Commandments, as my parents and pastor laid their hands on my head and shoulders, I claimed the faith in which I was raised was now my own.

As a part of that service, a Scripture passage was read from Luke 4:18–19. I had picked the text out of a list of suggestions. I liked the way it sounded. It seemed relevant for confirmation, when I was being blessed into adulthood and claiming my faith for myself—a continuation of the baptismal promises my parents and my church had made.

Little did I know how relevant that passage would be to my life. Luke 4:18–19 reads,

> The Spirit of the Lord is upon me,
>> because he has anointed me
>>> to bring good news to the poor.
> He has sent me to proclaim release to the captives
>> and recovery of sight to the blind,
>>> to let the oppressed go free,
> to proclaim the year of the Lord's favor.

One fascinating tidbit is that this passage is not original to Luke. It is printed in Luke because Jesus reads it out loud from the scroll of the prophet Isaiah when he visits his hometown. The passage from Isaiah goes on much longer than what is given in Luke,[1] but Jesus begins his preaching on this text by saying, "Today, the scripture has been fulfilled in your hearing." Jesus's visit to his hometown synagogue goes downhill from there, eventually ending with the people attempting to throw him off a cliff.

And yet that passage from Isaiah has continued to have relevance for advocates through the centuries, and especially for me. When I selected it for my confirmation, I didn't realize how formative it would be. And yet here I am, over three decades later, following a call from the Spirit of the Lord to bring good news to the poor and liberty to the captives as a Lutheran deacon working professionally as an LGBTQ advocate.

I still think it's strange that I'm an LGBTQ advocate. I never considered LGBTQ advocacy as a possible vocation—until it became an inevitable calling. Some of my earliest affirmations as a gay man came from my church, something I now realize is not common. I found no conflict between my LGBTQ identity and my Christian faith. I had even turned a few skeptics into tentative allies. Reaching people to change their perspectives felt good. Affirming, even. I assumed it was my natural charm and charisma that challenged anti-LGBTQ attitudes. I could simply deploy that charm and charisma to make the rest of the world accept, if not the whole LGBTQ community, at least me.

My egotistic winning streak of changing hearts and minds ended after college, when I joined a traveling musical ministry program that turned out to be staunchly anti-LGBTQ. Affirming people were involved, but they could not outweigh the overarching policies and culture that saw LGBTQ people as abominations. That conflict was reflected within the team I traveled with as well as the hierarchy of the organization. Eventually, the president of the organization decided to remove me from ministry with the program. The charm and charisma I had counted on didn't win the right people over. I was kicked out, and the organization remained unchanged.

That personal experience facing homophobia opened my eyes to the pervasiveness and perseverance of discrimination in our world and fundamentally shifted my vocation. I realized that even with all my privilege, I couldn't prevent experiencing prejudice myself. That made me start to think about the many other people who are facing the discrimination I had been fortunate to be shielded against.

I knew I needed to do something. But what? I was never formally trained in advocacy, and I had a privileged, midwestern, conflict-avoidant aversion to putting myself into any boot camp–style training that could teach me the skills necessary for community organizing and movement building. Over time, though, I was given opportunities and invitations to bring my skills and gifts to LGBTQ and social justice movements as a volunteer, a board member, and eventually a staff person. I spent time in the LGBTQ advocacy movement learning from others, making mistakes, and developing a strategic mindset about how to advance justice in this world.

While I learned a lot about strategy and advocacy, I also realized that my knowledge and skills were helpful to the movement. I used my education and experience in youth ministry to build programs like the Naming Project, which focuses on creating a faithful community for LGBTQ youth. I organized conferences for ReconcilingWorks, where people strategized and trained for creating a more inclusive church. I've been a board chair as well as a phone banker. I tried and failed to be a campaign door knocker.

I didn't think of what I was doing as advocacy. To me, it was just filling a need. Once, at a conference, I confided to someone that I didn't claim the word *activist* for myself because I didn't see my work that way. I described my ministry with LGBTQ youth through the Naming Project as well as my work with ReconcilingWorks, helping congregations make a statement of welcome. She listened to me patiently and then looked at me directly and said, "I think what you are describing sounds exactly like what an activist would do."

My advocacy has also led me to support and volunteer and collaborate with other movements focused on economic, racial, and environmental justice. Through that support and collaboration, I learned how much our movements are related. The sins of white supremacy, patriarchy, and exploitation often are the sources of the inequality and oppression we see today. The skills to combat those sins can apply to multiple movements at the same time.

DON'T GET DESPONDENT

This world can be pretty overwhelming. There is so much happening that can take our time, energy, and attention. Many things trouble our hearts and occupy our minds. Our worries might be personal—for example, financial concerns about stretching budgets or stress about our own health or the health of loved ones. The news constantly feeds us worries about our country. We continue to see violence being used as a tool of oppression, attacking teachers, doctors, nurses, government workers, drag queens, people of color, LGBTQ people, and so many more. The political process intended to meet our national needs feels either inadequate to address our current climate or like it actively contributes to advancing the hostility through policy. Around the world, we hear stories of war, persecution, hunger, corruption, and people forced to leave their homeland in search of safety.

There is a lot more I'm not mentioning explicitly. There are probably things that you are thinking about as well. Our hearts and our minds can be filled with a sense of overwhelmedness, unable to fathom any bigger picture about what God is doing in the world because we just see trauma and pain.

As Christians, we are all called and anointed to bring good news to the poor, release to the captives, and freedom to the oppressed. That commandment is clear in both the Hebrew Scriptures and the words of Jesus. Just as the problems of this world are interconnected, so are the solutions. God created us with a diverse set of identities, skills, and social locations and put us in relationships with one another. These relationships cause us to care about issues beyond ourselves.

From this book, I want everyday Christians, "real people," to understand our individual and collective calling to justice and start to think strategically and take practical steps to live justice out on a daily basis. I believe many of us truly want to live out that calling in our everyday lives, but often our fears and insecurities hold us back. It's important to address those fears directly, so we'll go through them here.

We can be easily trapped by the comforts of our privileged lives and don't want to disrupt the way things are working for us.

Jesus told a parable about a man whose crops performed exceptionally well. The man's main concern was how to safely keep all that grain for himself.[2] We may feel very differently about our personal futures than we do about our collective future. Often, the personal future wins.

It's tempting to compare ourselves to someone whom we think is doing advocacy better. We have some great heroes in the history of advocacy, people who have become nearly folkloric. Names like Martin Luther King Jr. and Mahatma Gandhi ring large in our memories, and we ask ourselves how we can possibly live up to their example. Even today, we see large-scale protests and actions and wonder if we would have the fortitude of those people.

We may get hung up on how to do advocacy "correctly." Too often, we've been passive, waiting to be told what to do, wanting to know we can do it perfectly before we even try, scared of our personal repercussions for messing up. Worst of all, we may fear accidentally causing more harm than good by doing it wrong.

One last fear that can hold us back is that dirty word *politics*. We live in a moment in history when every action, every phenomenon has become politicized. It can become easy to see an action as partisan when instead it is trying to solve a particular problem. The toxicity of politics creates anxiety about taking action. I don't want this to be seen as a political book, but policy—and by extension politics—is how we get a lot of this stuff done. I will offer tactics to live out progressive values that honor God's creation and to love our neighbors in our personal and communal lives.

As Christians, it is our job to view every action and phenomenon as theological, asking where God is and what we are being called to do. Sometimes God is calling us to direct service through food pantries, disaster response, and even the occasional mission trip. Other times we are called to end oppression, in all its forms, through policy or cultural change.

One goal of this book is to identify these barriers to the calling of advocacy and start to overcome them in our own spirit and among the communities to which we belong, including our churches. We can also decrease the anxiety about what to do and take away the fear of doing it wrong.

MAKE IT PRACTICAL

I am going to attempt to make this book as practical as possible, but I will need your help in two ways to make that happen. The first is for you to take what I'm saying and translate it into the particular issue or issues on your heart today. Since most of my work has been within the LGBTQ movement, that's where many of the stories and examples will come from, but the mindset and the skills we are going to discuss can be applied to many areas of progressive justice in service of the gospel. Heck, someone could use these skills to advocate for values and positions I don't support. In fact, many of these skills have been used by people on many different sides of each issue. I can't apply every principle to every context. That task will have to be up to you. To help you do that, I have put a "Reflection and Action" section at the end of each chapter, and my second ask is that you take these sections seriously. These exercises will help you think about the issues you are working on, both strategically and theologically. You will also be given some actions to take to ensure we aren't just talking about justice but acting on it. Let the "Reflection and Action" sections be moments when you apply what you have read to your own life and your own context.

My hope is that this book will inspire you to feel the anointing by the Holy Spirit, to live out the call to faithful advocacy in your own life, and to find real, tangible ways that you live out those values, sometimes through the simple decisions you make and sometimes by taking bold steps beyond your comfort zone. You are probably already aware of the injustice that still reigns in our world. I am hoping that by sharing a bit of what I've learned, you will discern how God is calling you to respond faithfully.

1 | INHERIT YOUR CALLING TO JUSTICE

I held my fortieth birthday party at the Stonewall Inn in New York City. Yes, the same Stonewall Inn where in 1969 a three-day riot—led by transgender women, drag queens, and queer people of color—launched what is credited to be the modern LGBTQ movement. The Stonewall uprising birthed several LGBTQ organizations, including the Street Transvestite Action Revolutionaries, the Gay Liberation Front, the Gay Activists Alliance, and even Parents and Friends of Lesbians and Gays.[1] Even after being named a national monument, the Stonewall Inn is still a functioning bar, with a pool table on the first floor and a stage for performances on the second.[2]

One block away from the Stonewall is Julius', a lesser-known historic watering hole. Three years before the Stonewall riots, the LGBTQ advocacy organization the Mattachine Society held a "sip-in" to challenge New York State Liquor Authority's prohibition on serving alcohol to LGBTQ people. Activists, pretty much all white men wearing suits and ties and followed by reporters and photographers from the local papers, entered Julius', announced they were gay, and asked to be served drinks.[3] The iconic photo from that day is of the bartender holding his hand over a glass to physically block alcohol from being poured into it. Today, over fifty years later, that photograph hangs on the wall of Julius'.

As a resident of New York City and an LGBTQ advocate, I've inherited the benefits of the actions at Julius' and Stonewall, including the ability to patronize both of these historic LGBTQ sites. After work, I regularly head to Julius' because it features a grill, serving delicious burgers, hot dogs, and onion rings. The Stonewall has often been a setting for my personal advocacy. In 2011, I was crowded inside the Stonewall watching the televisions broadcasting the New York State legislature's legalization of marriage equality. Later, through my work at GLAAD, I was on a planning team organizing a rally for the moment when the Supreme Court would release its decision to strike down or uphold the Defense of Marriage Act and Proposition 8. One of the owners of the Stonewall was also on the planning call, telling us, "You can do it on the street in front of our place. Everyone just comes there anyway when historic LGBTQ moments happen." Two years later, we organized another rally in front of the Stonewall after the Supreme Court ruled that marriage equality is a right under the equal protection clause of the Fourteenth Amendment to the Constitution.[4]

The LGBTQ movement enjoyed successes and endured devastating setbacks in the years following the Julius' sip-in and the Stonewall riots. While all this history was taking place, I was a child, closeted and dealing with bullying and rejection by my peers, oblivious to the struggles happening that would impact my future. Even though I'm an heir of the previous generations of the LGBTQ movement's activism, I learned about Stonewall only after growing up, coming out, and getting involved in the LGBTQ movement for myself. I didn't learn about Julius' until after I moved to New York City, well into my personal history of activism.

USE OUR HISTORY TO BUILD OUR ADVOCACY

Part of the experience of getting involved in advocacy is realizing that you missed the beginning of the struggle for justice. We must recognize we have often taken for granted the benefits that have been passed down through others' actions. I've often felt like I'm stepping into a movie that is two-thirds over, just getting to see the ending. I'm sometimes left with the feeling that the victories the LGBTQ community secured were not truly for me. They were for those who had gone before and experienced higher levels of discrimination at a time when our culture and laws were much less accepting and protective of the LGBTQ community.

I wonder if that's how previous generations of activists felt when they were finding ways to challenge injustice. Did the members of the Mattachine Society know that their legacy would include a photo of the sip-in hanging on the wall at Julius' over fifty years later? Could they imagine Julius' would be a setting for films and television series that tell the story of LGBTQ history, from *Love Is Strange*, to *Pose*, to *Can You Ever Forgive Me?*

Go and Do Likewise: The Stonewall Inn and Julius' are both LGBTQ historical venues in New York City. Research the history of the issue you are working on. Who have been the leaders? Where are some historical landmarks? If possible, visit those historic sites to study the history of the movement you are connected with. What you learn about the movement's history will inform your work today.

Did the rioters at Stonewall imagine that future generations of LGBTQ people would continue to gather inside the bar in times of celebration and times of peril for the LGBTQ community? Did they know they were creating a historical legacy that would be passed down from generation to generation? Or were they simply trying to survive yet another instance of police and societal harassment, something LGBTQ people and people of color have continuously faced in different forms over the decades? Did they think their circumstances were any more or less dire than what gender nonconforming, queer people of color had endured in the generations before them?

What about us today? Do we realize that we are just as much a part of history as those people we've studied from generations past? Or do we think our lives are mundane compared to what previous generations had to endure? Even our churches can tend toward building communities that are safe and comfortable. But when we look around, we realize that we are living in extraordinary times and called to live out heroic lives, just like the judges and prophets of the Hebrew Scripture, the disciples of the New Testament, or the saints over the ages. None of them realized they were called to great things, and they had no idea that their stories, or at least versions of their stories, would live on after they were gone. They were simply doing what needed to be done in the moment.

Each generation of biblical heroes, saints, and present-day advocates draws upon the previous generation's accomplishments. The Bible is the ongoing story of the relationship between God and humanity, how that relationship grows and changes and evolves with each succeeding generation. We can see the thread that runs through each person, each psalm, each parable, and each action. If we pay attention, we can see that same thread running through our lives, calling us to step up in the same way as those before us. Paul even acknowledges as much in his Letter to the Corinthians, where he states, "I planted, Apollos watered, but God gave the growth."[5] God uses our intergenerational efforts to build upon what has been passed along to us and prepare the next generation to take our work to heights we could never have imagined.

REMEMBER YOUR OWN CONVERSION MOMENTS

Our calling to social justice work happens at a particular time and place for each of us. We cannot let timing—thoughts that we are too late—hold us back from acting. We cannot let our past inaction or even opposition to a particular justice movement prevent us from learning, growing, and speaking out and acting against injustice, even the past injustices in which we participated.

Many of the most compelling social justice leaders have had their own "conversion moments" that stirred them out of complacency and into action. Or they may have had the realization that they were on the wrong side of an issue and changed their viewpoint completely. Our biblical heroes often have their own conversion moments. Consider Paul, a onetime persecutor of the followers of Jesus, who has his "road to Damascus" experience that turns him into a zealous defender of Jesus Christ. That experience drives him to join the early Christian movement, the very movement he had been violently persecuting. Paul is a latecomer to Christianity. He never meets Jesus or hears his teachings, nor does he witness his death and resurrection.

And yet Paul has the zeal of a convert, stepping into the Christian movement after so many others had suffered and even given their lives. Perhaps Paul feels regret at having been on the wrong side of history and feels a desire to make up for it. He uses his specific moment in history to his advantage, recognizing that he cannot change what came before him. Paul turns to arguing with his former colleagues, the Pharisees. He supports new worshipping communities beyond the scope of what had previously existed.

Paul moves the Christian movement along, helping it evolve from the ragtag disciples who had direct experiences with Jesus into the church that generations have inherited, including us.

I've been calling these social justice efforts "movements," and the metaphor of a movement is apt.[6] None of us was present at the beginning of the movement toward justice, since it began when God spoke the heavens and earth into being. We enter into this movement when we join our actions to the collective actions of the cloud of witnesses who came before us. Eventually, we pass this movement along to the next generation. They will receive the gift of our advances and encounter new challenges that we never had to face.

REFLECTION AND ACTION

Reflect: This chapter's "Go and Do Likewise" asked you to start thinking about history. What's the history behind the movement you are feeling called to support?

Act: Spend some time researching who has worked on this before you and who is working on it now.

Reflect: How does your movement show up in Scripture?

Act: Find a Scripture passage that informs your advocacy on a particular issue. (Trust me, this will come in handy later.)

Reflect: Why are you feeling called to this particular movement at this particular time?

Act: Write it down.

Reflect: What do you hope happens as a result of your participation?

Act: Write it down on that same piece of paper from the last question.

2 | DON'T REMAIN ISOLATED. GET CONNECTED.

It is not good that the man should be alone.[1]

Those words are just as true for us now as they were when God uttered them about Adam in the garden of Eden. Connection is vital for our well-being and our longevity in this work. It provides encouragement when we are timid, perspective when we overthink, and companionship so that we know we are not alone. Connection also amplifies our advocacy, turning our lone actions into something that cannot be ignored.

I grew up in northern Minnesota, along the Canadian border. To say that I had an isolated upbringing is a massive understatement. The population of the town I grew up in was only about eight hundred, and I lived fifteen miles outside town. Our house was five miles beyond the end of the telephone lines, meaning we didn't have a phone in the house until technology allowed "car phones." For a good portion of my childhood, we only had Canadian television. For the longest time, I thought I was Canadian, since that was all the media I was consuming.

Of course, I was also a gay boy living in a small town with no other openly LGBTQ people in the 1980s and 1990s. When I started to recognize my feelings at a young age, I had no language, no role models, no examples of what it meant to be gay. As I got older, I did get messages about what it meant, and it wasn't anything good. It was the object of bullying. It was depicted by the dying AIDS patients we saw on our evening news. It was also something that was seen as happening in big cities, far away from my little town.

That sense of isolation kept me in the closet throughout my entire youth. Even after I started telling people I was gay, I could only talk about what I was thinking or feeling, trying to explain it to others. I still didn't have role models to show me the joys and challenges facing the LGBTQ community.

Today, I'm an LGBTQ advocate, but I had a long, slow learning curve. I didn't know what parts of my experiences were unique to me and which were common. In the 1980s and 1990s, thanks to those images we saw being broadcast from major cities, to be gay meant dying an early death from AIDS. It wasn't until I left my hometown that I got some sense of the larger LGBTQ community.

After I had moved away, come out, and established my life in a larger city, surrounded by other LGBTQ people to give me some perspective, I read an obituary for my hometown's former mayor. The obituary ran in an LGBTQ publication, describing the contributions he had made to the LGBTQ movement in Minnesota and hailing him as an LGBTQ community leader. It even mentioned a life partner and a daughter I never knew existed. I had no idea that there was a gay man in my own local community. I didn't feel safe coming out, and I'm certain he didn't either.

This sense that we are the only ones recognizing or being impacted by a particular injustice can hinder us from even speaking up in the first place and prevents so many movements from advancing. The stigma that keeps people from speaking up about their personal struggles also keeps them from connecting with others who face the same obstacles for mutual support or strategic thinking. Additionally, others don't learn about these issues because they aren't exposed to the stories of marginalized communities and don't realize the scope of the problems. When we don't talk about issues or if they are perceived to be far away and experienced by people removed from our lives, we become fooled into thinking that our systemic issues are just personal anomalies.

The book of John describes Jesus's encounter with a woman experiencing the same type of isolation. She is going to the well in the midst of the midday sun. She is alone, not traveling in the company of other women. We don't know the full reasons for this, although since Jesus mentions her five husbands, it may be due to sexual shaming. She is isolated, with no one to support her or even offer encouragement.

After having a profound conversation with Jesus, this woman runs back to town to tell others. She has been changed through this encounter with Jesus, and she wants to bring others into the experience. The first thing she says to her community is a combination of a statement and a question: "Come and see a man who told me everything I have ever done! He cannot be the Messiah, can he?"[2] She needs someone else to check her perspective, to confirm if what she heard and experienced might be true outside of her own head and heart.

At its best, your community might corroborate your concerns or your experience. Even if the people aren't having the same experience, a good, caring community stands by you as you process what you are thinking and feeling, helping you form a strategy and supporting you in the action. The woman at the well could have just kept her encounter to herself, but then nothing would have come of it. Instead, she became an accidental evangelist just by sharing what happened to her and inviting others to experience Jesus for themselves and confirm her impression of him.

At its worst, your community might commit gaslighting; it could ignore, downplay, or outright deny your perception and experiences. The town easily could have refused to listen to or believe the woman at the well. The people could have scolded her for talking to a stranger, chalking it up to her loose morals. We have countless examples through history and contemporary culture of denying the struggles and concerns of others. Effective gaslighting from the people around you leads you to think no one else is experiencing the same thing you are, that you are the only one who perceives an injustice. When you can't share your concerns about the status quo with others, then you may accept the current reality as "just the way it is" and not feel moved to advocate for change. You don't know any better. It takes interactions with others who are also seeing an injustice the way you are to form strategic solutions on how to fix it.

REACH OUT TO OTHERS WHO MAY FEEL THE SAME ISOLATION

Sometimes, the impetus for advocacy is the sense of isolation itself. Conie Borchardt is a musician, entrepreneur, community builder, storyteller, and everyday advocate. Several years after we graduated from college, I reconnected with her at the Parliament of the World's Religions, where she was using music and movement to enable community and storytelling. Since then, I've witnessed her develop several initiatives intended to confront and heal trauma. As a Twin Cities resident, she held a livestreamed vigil on the traumatic nights after George Floyd's murder. That's the sort of spirit she has.

Conie grew up on a farm in rural southern Minnesota with a white father and an Asian mother. Her town was overwhelmingly white, and the dominant culture of whiteness, what can be called white supremacy, can either ignore or persecute difference, leaving a sense of isolation and differentness that builds into internalized trauma.

Conie told me that as an adult, she searched for a community that shared her identity and experience. She attended the Midwest Mixed Conference, a gathering for people with mixed racial identities. Conie said it was the first time she had been around such a large group of others who grew up as mixed-race people in the white-dominated culture that permeates the Upper Midwest. It gave her a feeling that she wasn't alone and that the experiences she had were validated by hearing other people's stories.

Conie returned the following year to continue enjoying that sense of connection with others of a similar experience. At her second conference, she began noticing some nuance between her identity and that of the conference leadership. Very few of the conference leaders were Asian, and the conference participants who were Asian were largely transnational adoptees. Conie heard stories about being biracial from a Black perspective, and she heard stories about being Asian in a white-dominated culture, but she was also aware of the nuance of her personal identity and experience and how that differed from others at the conference.

After the murders of Philando Castile and George Floyd in Minneapolis, Conie was impressed by the significant level of organizing in the Black community. She supported their efforts, but it inspired a longing to build a community of solidarity for biracial Asian people who had their own unique forms of trauma. This led Conie to the realization that she wanted to be around and share her experiences with other mixed-race Asian people, especially those who came from rural communities. For Conie, it was the impetus to share her story in search of others who might relate.

Conie drew upon her experience as a song leader and as a facilitator to launch different initiatives. One is Biracial and Rural, what Conie describes as "a community of care and story-telling space where BIPOC (Black, indigenous, people of color) voices in current and past rural spaces are nurtured and empowered to build sustaining communal resources going forward."[3] The aim of Biracial and Rural is to build connections of mutual support and understanding to heal from and eventually combat the internalized trauma that comes with living as a minority in a rural area. The main organizing principle for Biracial and Rural is storytelling in many different forms, including poetry, song, movement, and retreats where people can discuss and share their experiences. Ongoing check-ins sustain the community of support and care after the time together.

Another related and complimentary initiative is Freeing Refrains. In 2021, this was a virtual retreat (like so many things that were virtual) that created a storytelling space for participants to examine what is binding us and what is freeing us. Of the six gatherings, five were held for BIPOC people, while the sixth was open to all. It provided a space for processing and healing. The gatherings also built stronger connections among participants, who were still living and functioning in a world filled with racism, trauma, and gaslighting.

Community builds resilience and motivates us to engage in an otherwise hostile world. But the benefits stretch far beyond personal well-being. It also helps us recognize gaslighting—when we experience it and when we perpetuate it onto others. By being in community, we can better understand generational trauma and why so-called microaggressions are rooted in long-running patterns of behavior. It allows us to be better neighbors to those who come from places of difference.

LOOK INTO JOINING AN EXISTING ORGANIZATION

The easiest way to connect with others who care about your particular issue is to join an existing organization. Consider joining a national organization that has a local chapter. You have the benefit of a larger scope, an overall strategy, and resources that come from a centralized source, but you have the flexibility to adapt all that to your local context. You'll work with your neighbors who know the culture of your state or community, with the added benefit of expanding your circle of friends and acquaintances. If no chapter exists, start one. If no organization exists that addresses the nuance you need, follow Conie's example to create your own.

One example from the political sphere is this: Indivisible is a progressive political organization formed after the 2016 election. Two former Capitol Hill staffers wrote a document about effective political engagement based on their experience of being on the receiving end of Tea Party activism during the 2010s.

They posted the document, which they called a manifesto, on the internet, where it went viral.[4]

The Indivisible manifesto, as it was called, caught on, as local community activists, fired up from the 2016 election results, used it as a template for action with their own elected leaders. People met to encourage one another and coordinate elected leader outreach, which eventually led to Indivisible chapters forming all over the country. It's easier to take actions like calling elected leaders or making office visits when you know you aren't doing them alone. This coordination also allows people to amplify their actions, creating visible crowds at public events and further reach as each member shares photos and messages on social media.

Richard and I joined our local Indivisible chapter in the fall of 2020. Having a local chapter makes doing political advocacy easier. As a group, we interpret the manifesto guidance in the context of our local community and our specific elected leaders, from the president down to our city council members. But the best value is meeting and connecting with neighbors who know the neighborhood issues and local politics. They are fun people who pair progressive values with socializing in the park, at someone's home, or at a local restaurant. After a year with our local Indivisible group, I felt more informed about my city and state than I had for the previous ten years I lived there. One of the things said at the beginning of my local Indivisible meetings is, "All are welcome here, however or how much you can fit activism in your life. Just coming to meetings is a powerful act of resistance!"

MAKE OUR CHURCHES COMMUNITY CONNECTORS

Our churches can also be centers for meeting, framing news and current events through the lens of our Christian faith, and living out our calling "to bring good news to the poor . . . recovery of sight to the blind, to let the oppressed go free."[5] We can host Bible studies that connect the news of the day with relevant themes within Scripture. We can organize group visits with elected leaders, amplifying our voices and bringing our faith into the public realm. Many of our congregations have built social ministries: food pantries, preschools, and so on. Through these ministries, we encounter people from the community. While our congregational social ministry provides direct service, we can encourage civic engagement in a nonpartisan way. We can invite people to sign petitions about the issues related to our ministries; guide people through the process of registering to vote, even in a nonpartisan manner; and every ten years, help people complete census forms.

> **Go and Do Likewise:** Find out if your congregation is part of a faith-based advocacy network. These organizations connect faith leaders with advocacy opportunities around given issues. Some are state-specific, while others are national. You can find a list of such organizations at the end of the book. Sign up yourself or your congregation (if you have permission). Participate in their actions and use their resources.

Perhaps your church is a part of one of many faith-based social justice networks around the country. Ask if your church is involved with any such organization or if there are existing advocacy priorities for the congregation. Ask your congregational leaders if they are personally involved with an advocacy organization and if you can join them. Doing your work with others will make you stronger and leverage any action you take.

If your congregation isn't doing social justice work in any formal way, then you have a few options:

1. Push your congregation to get involved in social justice work.

2. Form your own informal network.

3. Go it alone.

Numbers one and two are not mutually exclusive. You don't have to wait for your congregation to formally get involved, but you might form your own network that leads your congregation into meaningful action. There may be times when we will be called to go it alone, but that is the least desirable option, leading to the isolation described at the beginning of this chapter.

Your advocacy organization doesn't have to be formal. It can happen casually—in community with others who share your values. Small groups, book clubs, dinner parties, or wine nights with others who have an interest in the same advocacy that you do will help you all encourage one another. The important thing is not to just talk about the issues but to create a plan for what to do.

In an effort to build a more tight-knit, intentional community, my husband and I have hosted game nights. We've invited between six and ten friends over for hors d'oeuvres and a selection of games. But before we begin the games, we hand out supplies to write letters for Vote Forward,[6] a program that identifies infrequent voters who appear on voter rolls in key states. The letters provide templates with the opportunity to send personal messages to voters, reminding them that voting is essential to our democracy and encouraging them to vote in the next upcoming election. We ask all the friends at our game nights to write ten letters before we start eating, drinking, and playing board games.

One note of caution: don't let the gatherings be the end of the advocacy process. They are intended to encourage you and your guests and perhaps help formulate a strategy for action. Don't just read a book about antiracism. Identify the action steps that you will take to work for antiracism in your church, community, school, or work. We want to take informed action, considering what is the best, most strategic next step to take in our pursuit of justice. The book of James says, "Faith by itself, if it has no works, is dead."[7] I say, "Book clubs without action don't save democracy."

Communities are not perfect. After all, they are made up of humans who are in bondage to sin. But isolation is usually worse, as it can hold us back from using the gifts and passions God gave us to meet the needs of the world. Find folks who share your passions and who want to find a way to do something. Get connected, and then act.

REFLECTION AND ACTION

Reflect: Is there something on your heart or mind about which you feel isolated, something you feel you cannot talk about with the people you interact with on a daily basis?

Act: Seek out a community with which you can talk about this issue. It may take an internet search or going to people outside your immediate network of contacts.

Reflect: Is your congregation a part of a faith-based community organizing network? If so, how much do you know about it?

Act: Have a conversation with your church leaders about the congregation's participation in advocacy.

Reflect: Who, among the people God has placed in your life, has passions for some of the same areas of advocacy as you?

Act: Schedule a one-on-one conversation with them about their passions.

Reflect: What could secular advocacy organizations have to teach your congregation or network of peers? How could your congregation enhance the work of secular advocacy organizations?

Act: Invite a representative from a secular advocacy organization to present on their work. This could be at your congregation or at your home. The idea is to build a community that cares about this issue as much as you do.

3 | SPEAK UP.
DON'T STAY SILENT.

When the news and our social media feeds are saturated with an onslaught of troubling reports of violence, corruption, and degradation, it's easy to simply shake our heads and move on with our own tasks and worries. This is especially true when what is being reported feels out of our control or far removed from our everyday lives. In this chapter, I'm going to urge you to resist that temptation. When we hear the news of a broken, sinful world, where injustice has power, we need to think strategically about what we can do or say. We can commiserate with our like-minded peers about the terrible state of the world. However, at some point, someone is going to have to take these concerns outside our bubble.

If no one says or does anything, nothing changes. That's why it's up to us. We have already decided that a particular issue, whatever it is, is important. Maybe it's fair wages for workers, climate change, gender equality, or the securing of democracy. Once we've learned about it, it's hard to shake the feeling that we are called to do something about it. That is God's calling placed upon our hearts. So we spend time in study and prayer. We learn more, which is part of the process. But eventually, we need to say or do something.

Saying something is uncomfortable. I'm of Scandinavian heritage and very conflict avoidant. The temptation to stay silent just to avoid uncomfortable conversations is strong. It is also hard for me to form the words to adequately articulate my opinion in the moment. I need time to think through what I want to say. If this is also you, I hope you can relate to my experience.

USE YOUR PUBLIC STATEMENTS TO INVITE PRIVATE CONVERSATIONS

As Christians, we follow a vocal leader who was unafraid to proclaim uncomfortable truths. Jesus brought words of comfort to the poor and marginalized. He denounced the unholy alliance between religion and the politics of his day. In doing so, he angered powerful religious and political leaders. Besides his proclamations, he took action. We are talking about the guy who entered the temple to disrupt and throw out the vendors who were monetizing the people's faith. His words and actions put him in the crosshairs of the religious and political authorities. The religious leaders of the day both condemned him publicly and complained about him privately.

But even among all the peer pressure to condemn Jesus outright, one religious leader was intrigued and wanted to learn more. Nicodemus approached Jesus in the middle of the night.[1] I suspect Nicodemus was genuinely interested in what Jesus had to say. He had sincere questions that he didn't want to ask in front of the others. As a Pharisee, he was dealing with peer pressure to reject Jesus and his message. He had to approach Jesus by night, away from his peers.

We might think this clandestine conversation between Nicodemus and Jesus is extraordinary. But this dynamic happens much more often than we think. We spend a lot of time discussing issues privately rather than speaking or acting on them publicly.

In 2009, my denomination, the Evangelical Lutheran Church in America, lifted its ban on LGBTQ relationships and clergy at a dramatic Churchwide Assembly. Following that action, several churches tried to withdraw from the denomination, and more than a few succeeded. Congregations were divided, with members who both supported and opposed LGBTQ inclusion in the church. Those who wanted to leave the denomination over this issue were often loud, overwhelming any other opinion. Congregational meetings commonly included ranting about LGBTQ people and bullying those who supported their inclusion.

Speaking up at one of these meetings in support of the denomination's action and LGBTQ people was a very intimidating experience. And yet people did it. They reported back to me the fear they felt when they tentatively stood up to speak in support of LGBTQ people. Some described their voices shaking. Then following the meetings, they were approached by others, often clandestinely, whispering, "I agree with you." Just like Nicodemus approached Jesus, others approached them to ask more questions, get more information, share their concerns, and get some caring, nuanced answers.

Did Nicodemus speak up for Jesus later? Did Jesus inspire him? We don't know. But if Jesus had not been speaking up—proclaiming the kingdom of God and raising legitimate concerns about the abusive practices of religion that pull us away from God—Nicodemus would have likely been swept along with the sentiment of his fellow Pharisees, believing whatever was being said about Jesus and having no opportunity to learn firsthand about what Jesus was saying.

Go and Do Likewise: When we are aware of the difficulty in speaking up, we also need to offer support to those who do so. If you can, vocalize your support in the moment to demonstrate visible allyship for the person who has broken the ice to speak the uncomfortable truth. If that is not possible, the next best option is to follow the example of Nicodemus and have a follow-up conversation with the person who spoke up. Offer your support and ask what they need from you in the moment.

BE AWARE OF THE RISKS OF SPEAKING UP

I just spent a chapter talking about the feeling of isolation. That isolation can be broken only after someone speaks up.

Of course, sticking our necks out comes with risks. Speaking out can leave us ostracized. I hate to say this, but speaking publicly about our values can make us targets for harassment, vandalism, and violence. I don't want to minimize the risk because it exists. We can't use the example of Jesus without remembering that he was arrested and executed.

The more privilege you have, the more ability you have to speak out and weather the repercussions. It is often afforded to people in the dominant culture; you've probably heard of white privilege and male privilege. Privilege here simply means that you have been afforded trust, resources, and influence that make speaking up less risky. You may have additional social power, networks of support, and even money to mitigate any long-term damage.

Instead of feeling guilty about privilege or using it for personal gain, you can use it to speak up in public settings, calling out what is wrong and lifting up the ideas and voices of those who are more vulnerable by speaking out. You may already be in rooms where others can't reach: C-suite offices, board or council meetings, or the homes of influential figures. If you have privilege, use it to your advantage and to the advantage of those who cannot speak out.

We speak up because others often cannot. Your decision to speak out may carry less risk than that of others who may be financially, socially, emotionally, or even physically vulnerable. For some, just existing is a revolutionary act of bravery. We can support that bravery by speaking up when we see injustice, naming sin as sin, and calling for a better and more just world.

MITIGATE THE RISKS OF SPEAKING UP

We have ways that we can mitigate the risks for ourselves. Prepare yourself as much as you can for the moment when you will speak up in a group or public setting. Have as many individual conversations with as many supporters or potential supporters as you're able. Preparing with your support network can do a few important things.

It provides you with the moral support that will give you encouragement and strength. Having had those individual conversations is going to strengthen your resolve. It reminds you that you are not speaking into a hostile void but supported by people who believe in the same values as you. It will break the sense of isolation that could keep you from mustering the strength to speak up.

The other thing that speaking to individual supporters does is allow you to practice what you want to say and how you want to say it. For many of us, the words do not come naturally, especially when the pressure is on. Talking to others is a way to form a mental script for yourself. Their feedback can help you hone your words to have the most impact and power. The questions and challenges from your supporters and loved ones can help you prepare for more hostile questions and challenges. Practicing with others you know also helps you learn your words by heart, so you can speak from your heart.

CONSIDER THE TRUE IMPACT OF SOCIAL MEDIA

The most convenient way to speak out is on social media. There are memes, graphics, videos, and written pieces out there that perhaps articulate the issue better than we can. It's easy to want to pass along other people's thoughts. Sometimes, that's the simplest thing to do. Easy peasy. One and done.

However, easy isn't always effective. In fact, there is limited value in posting on social media. You are most likely to reach your closest circle of connections, people like your family and closest friends. For those of us who aren't famous, most of our social media responses come from people with whom we have an existing real-world relationship. That means they are also largely, although not exclusively, people who hold the same values we do. If your closest social media followers are people who already agree with you, you may be adding to their knowledge base, but you aren't necessarily convincing them of anything—they are already convinced. Ideally, you reach people who are conflicted or unaware of the issue you are bringing up. Perhaps they believe it doesn't impact their lives or they want to avoid thinking about uncomfortable topics. Your posts might reach them and open their eyes to the realities you are describing.

As you consider all this, it's important to keep in mind that social media have a goal to keep people using the platforms as much as possible. Your message may not be seen by the people who have the most to learn from what you have to say. Social media platforms prioritize "engagement"—reactions and comments. The sentiment of those comments can be positive or negative (or even downright mean), but it all counts as "engagement." Generally, the most controversial posts get the most engagement, thereby rewarding the poster. So simply posting may not get your message in front of those who need to see it or who will react in a way that is helpful. You will need to go further.

Social media's prioritization of engagement means you will also need to be prepared for negative responses to your posts. How can you be prepared? First, know what your capacity for conflict is. Some people love to argue on social media, while others prefer to avoid it. Second, determine what sort of negative response it is. Is it a thoughtful argument against your position? Then you probably should respond and continue in the conversation. Others may be following the discussion and could learn something from witnessing a thoughtful debate. However, if the post is a personal attack or uses harmful language, you are well within your right to block and report the comment or the person. You are under no obligation to entertain someone who is engaging in bad faith and just making you feel bad about yourself and wasting your time.

One way to make your social media posts resonate with the audience that needs to see them is to add your own personal commentary. For example, even if you completely agree with an article you are sharing, you should summarize the sentiment in your own words, add your own personal story, or expand on the thoughts in the post. The personal addition lets people know that you actually read and thought about the article, even if they are unlikely to do so. It also makes the post personal, not just an idea you are passing on. You have analyzed and synthesized the information and expressed it through your own frame.

In addition to your own perspective or commentary on a post, include a call to action. Many people who see your post may be emotionally moved by what you share. This is the moment when they are most primed to take action. Give them a tangible one to take. It can be "Visit this website to learn more," "Donate," "Contact your representatives," "Share this," or whatever is most helpful to your cause.

A second way to make your social media posts go further and be seen by more people is to coordinate with peers to amplify one another's posts. Make a pact to comment, like, and share one another's posts on a given topic, each one adding their own additional commentary. You can even share articles and resources privately before you all share them at once, vetting and verifying helpful information out of the public eye. The mutual amplification makes posts even more visible to others, including mainstream media sources. You can join or create a Twitter direct message room, Facebook group, or text thread. You can also send an email to your network with sample social media messages, unifying hashtags, and even graphics to share. Some organizations create social media kits in Google Docs so they can be updated regularly. Prompting your network to share can keep the conversation on social media. If you want to take it a step further, collect the best posts and messages about your issue and share them with local reporters, including additional background information about the issue and what your organization is doing about it. The crossover of social media and traditional media reinforces the notion that people care about the issue and that they should be covering it.

FIND MULTIPLE WAYS TO SPEAK UP

Because of the limitations of social media, you will also need to speak up in many other ways. I cannot stress this enough. Simply posting online isn't going to be enough. It must be accompanied by real-world action, which is likely to have a much deeper and more lasting impact. Addressing an issue directly in front of others is much more effective but is also uncomfortable. It requires navigating some tension with others. But it's necessary.

The most impactful in-person scenario is face-to-face. If you can, meet with community and business leaders, clergy, and other decision makers to encourage them to take action in support of your advocacy. Talk to your elected leaders. As a constituent, you have a relationship, and you likely know more about the issue you are advocating for than they do. Use that relationship to teach them. Draw on your existing relationship—use the trust you've built—with the other person (or develop a new relationship, if needed) to help smooth over misconceptions and stereotypes. Like the conversation Nicodemus and Jesus had, this approach creates the opportunity to address confusion, concerns, and questions. You cannot address every hard question that comes your way, but you can be prepared to respond to as much as possible. This is where your preparation is going to come in handy.

Sometimes you will be called to make a more public statement in support of your values. Imagine being in a meeting, assembly, or conference. You may have a set amount of time to address your peers and decision makers and to convince them that the issue you care about should be one they care about as well or to propose a way you can take action together. As you prepare your statement, think about how others might respond and how you might reply. Visualizing and anticipating reactions, especially negative ones, can help you avoid being caught off guard, annoyed, hurt, and angry. Instead, the reaction can prompt you to give the response you had planned.

In other instances, you may be the one who can intervene and reason directly with an authority figure, such as a boss, elected official, community or business leader, or even local clergy. Privilege may make it easier and less risky for some to engage with people in these positions. The need to intervene might be required in the heat of the moment, when we see someone being treated unfairly. Or it might be needed to prevent that sort of treatment from happening in the first place. Bring your "I'd like to speak to the manager" energy, and use it for good, not evil.

Find other ways to get your message out there. Don't overlook the local and regional news. Letters to the editor are great ways to reach your local community and its leaders. Most letters to the editor are very short, often less than one hundred words, so you will have to be succinct. You can also send a story idea to reporters and editors, encouraging them to cover the issue. You then can provide background information to make covering that story easy. Of course, because you care, you should offer yourself to be interviewed or share a prewritten statement from you on the issue at hand.

No matter the situation, speaking up is going to be essential just to break the culture of silence. Perhaps you can reach people in a new or different way or you can personalize the issue so that folks can relate to it. There is risk. Yes, we can be scared of what can happen as a result of speaking up, but we can be even more scared of what sort of people we become when we stop standing up for our values.

REFLECTION AND ACTION

Reflect: Think about how you will need to prepare to speak up—something you need to learn, support you need to build, and so on.

Act: Start making a research plan and talking to your support system so you will be ready to speak up when the opportunity presents itself.

Act: Prepare your proactive talking points and what possible reactions you might get. Then prepare your responses to those reactions.

Reflect: What opportunities do you have to speak up? Individually? In a small-group setting? At a public meeting? In the media?

Act: Mark your calendar for the day you will speak up. Practice and prepare for that day the way a runner would practice for a marathon.

4 | BUILD ON PERSONAL RELATIONSHIPS

Frequently at my job at GLAAD, we hold crowdfunding campaigns. You are likely familiar with the format: We create individual webpages designed in a way that reflects our personalities and work. Then, we solicit our friends, family, and professional contacts for small and large donations.

Since fundraising is not a part of many of our regular job descriptions, our development team offers incentives, turning the campaign into a game, replete with prizes. Given that we all have different types of jobs, professional contacts, and social circles, the prizes reflect a diversity of actions taken. Prizes are given for the most creative page, most social media posts, best video appeal, and so on. But the constant prizes are in two categories: most money raised and most individual donations. The "most money raised" category is often won by people with higher net worth contacts, while the "most individual donations" category is often won by small donations from a wider pool of people. As the fundraising saying goes, every dollar counts.

My fundraising page isn't particularly spectacular. It is personalized, but there isn't anything on the page that would compel a random visitor to donate—which is fine because a random visitor isn't going to stumble onto my page anyway. People have to get to my page, and I have to provide them with the link.

Many of my colleagues post on social media, including a photo of them at work or at an event. I do too, but I rarely get donations solely through social media posts. Others send mass emails, with dozens of people on blind copy, often using the long, flowery language supplied by our development team.

For me, I find that a quick, direct appeal works best. I often send short direct messages, through either social media messaging or texting, asking for a donation. It is often as short and simple as "Hi, would you be willing to make a donation to my year-end fundraising for my organization?" with a link to my fundraising page.

In those short messages, I don't elaborate on the reasons for donating, explain the value of the work that we do at the organization, or even make the case. I simply ask for the donation. I spend a Friday afternoon, when my mind is just "done" with work, and scroll through either my Facebook friends or my phone's contact list. I find this is a good, mindless task that still benefits the organization.

There is an additional benefit. Often, I review my contact list just to make note of who I haven't communicated with in a while. If their last message from me was a fundraising appeal from the last campaign, I don't ask. If I know they are also fundraising for their own organizations, I don't ask. Instead, I send a note to say hello and that I am thinking of them. But as much as possible, I do ask for a donation. It often sparks conversation about what is happening in their lives. It is a way of reconnecting and keeping our relationship alive, even if I'm not asking them for something in that moment.

Go and Do Likewise: Organizations need as much help fundraising as possible. Beyond a direct donation, consider joining the fundraising efforts by creating your own mini-campaign. If your organization has a way, set up your own fundraising page. Otherwise, try any of the tools that raise money (GoFundMe, Facebook, etc.). Go beyond posting on social media. Make personal contact with friends, family, and even strangers. Keep it short and simple, allowing them the opportunity to support the same efforts as you.

The reason I don't make a lengthy case for a donation is that I try to keep people informed about my ongoing advocacy. I spend the year sharing about my work in various ways, and I work directly with many of the names in my contact list. They don't need a long, written-out argument that supporting my work is worthwhile because they often already value the work that I am doing.

If you need an analogy, it's a little like not having to pull an all-night study session to cram for a final exam because you have been doing the work throughout the semester. Some of my contacts are easily compelled into action. They know me and support my work because we have preexisting relationships. They are more inclined to give to me and my fundraising page rather than to a generic organizational page because they know and trust me. They know that supporting me with a donation is also establishing my value within the organization, beyond the fulfillment of my job description. The people aren't donating to the organization as much as they are donating to the relationships we have built. They are investing in me personally and hoping to see my work continue.

USE RELATIONSHIPS TO MAKE COMPLEX PROBLEMS MANAGEABLE

I'm using this fundraising story to highlight the importance of personal relationships in our advocacy work. Sometimes, the problems we want to solve seem gargantuan, bigger than what any of us can do by ourselves. We ask ourselves what we can do to provide dignity for migrants fleeing violence or to reduce global warming and the most devastating impacts of climate change. Our impacts will seem insignificant if we focus on what we can do alone. Pooling individual efforts with others will create a wider impact.

Starting with world leaders is pretty daunting, but we can influence our local and state leaders, especially those with whom we have an existing relationship and a certain level of influence. We will have a hard time convincing strangers of our position when they don't know us, our motivations, or our personality. They don't trust us until they know us.

But we do have local influence where people know us and our values. This includes the local pastors, city council, school board, business leaders, community elders, and so on. Even if you don't agree on important social or political issues, there is an affinity and a sense of commonality. You have influence with the people who know you best. Find ways to invoke mutually shared values and culture to talk about the issue you are advocating for. This doesn't always mean lecturing, yelling, or being preachy. It can mean finding ways to incorporate key ideas into conversations, finding a way to get them to look at your issue in a new light, one that will make sense to them.

The better you know these people, the more you can tailor your issues around their set of values. Let me be really clear, when trying to convince someone to come around to your point of view, you will need to frame your strategy and call to action within *their* worldview and values. It will take a little extra time and attention to figure out how to match their worldview, but the results will be well worth it.

In the next chapter, we'll think strategically about how to effectively reach and motivate your network of relationships. But for now, it's important to think through those people who have a connection to you and how you strengthen that connection in their minds and hearts. Think of the places you have lived. What's the local culture like? What are the local values? What are the local references you can incorporate into your vocabulary when you are asking people to do something?

MAP YOUR CIRCLE OF INFLUENCE

Maybe we don't have personal relationships with the decision makers who have the power to change policies and fix the problems we face. But we can think strategically about what audiences they do listen to. And we can start to build a web of relationships that can reach them.

Let's use an example: Imagine you want to change a state law. You may not have a personal relationship with the state lawmakers who will ultimately vote on this law. If you need to narrow it down, you will have stronger influence with an elected leader if you are their constituent. They want to keep you satisfied enough to vote for them in the next election cycle, or at least not vote against them. As a constituent, you have a shared geography, a shared understanding of the local values, and a shared interest in improvement for the area. You can start to build a relationship with the representative for your district based on those areas of commonality.

If you don't have the personal relationship to talk to the elected official directly, you can use the network of relationships they have. Who is in their first circle of influence? Who do they pay attention to? Who has influence over them?

Their fellow elected leaders?
Donors?
The media?
Political party members?
Local unions?
Local civic organizations and their leaders?
Local churches and faith leaders?

Take a closer look at that last item on the list. One of the local churches might be your congregation. Perhaps there are members who have closer connections to the elected leader than you do. Perhaps your fellow churchgoers are local civic leaders, donors, or political party influencers and your connection to the elected leader is through your congregation.

This list isn't exhaustive, but it's enough to get you started. I'll include a fuller worksheet at the end of this chapter. Think carefully about who your key target—in this case, the elected leader—pays attention to: individual names, organizations, and even titles.

After looking through the first circle of influence, create a second circle of influence. Who does that first circle pay attention to? Who might you know? Is there anyone with whom you have or can build a trusted relationship? If you need to create a third circle just to identify how you can build relationships with people in power, do it. It's a matter of finding the connections that can get to the decision makers.

Along the way, you build relationships with people, and there is no downside to relationship building. Maybe these people will be helpful to your advocacy in the future. Maybe they won't. As Christians, we see people not as tools to be used but as a network of relationships God has placed around us as a part of God's creation. These relationships can be grown and nurtured, even if you don't see an immediate way they can help your cause. Remember, just as much as you are advocating for a cause, the others with whom you are building relationships are also advocating for issues they care about, facing personal struggles, or just enjoying the companionship that comes with new friends. Your relationships may be mutually beneficial, separate from the issue you are advocating for. Might you be the person God is sending into their lives to help them through something? Conversely, God may be sending them into your life to help keep you better balanced and well rounded.

ASSESS YOUR RELATIONSHIP NETWORK AND EXPAND IT STRATEGICALLY

One pitfall of focusing on your own personal network is that you may soon realize that, in most instances, your social circle is filled with people of the same race, class, and ideology as you. This can be helpful in knowing what your community values, what they are scared of, what brings joy, and so on. But it also builds an echo chamber, lulling you into believing that the issues that are faced by your immediate social circle are the only ones out there or that your approach is the best (or only) way to solve a problem. That effect can lead white people to downplay the impact of racism because it's not impacting them or the people in their lives. Men often minimize sexism. Straight people don't realize the impact of homophobia. And even gay and lesbian people can overlook biphobia and transphobia in our world. I recognize this as a white gay man and how that influences the networks I'm a part of.

Do a very thorough and honest assessment of your privilege and perspective. This isn't intended to be punitive but rather allows you to recognize the gaps in your outlook. Then, seek out perspectives different from your own to learn what you aren't seeing, experiencing, and believing. This does not mean befriending someone for the sole purpose of making them into a teacher. Instead, find perspectives from those who are already teachers. Buy books and listen to podcasts from people who are working on a range of issues from various social positions. Take classes, take workshops, and pay those teachers who are working to impart perspective and education. Make it easier for them to live and make the world a better place. Build relationships where you listen to what is important to them rather than peppering them with questions that are important to you.

You will glean more perspective and strategy from their teaching, and you will also be challenged and pushed. This is all to make you a better advocate and ultimately to make our world a more just and loving place. It may also help you recognize the concerns of your friends, neighbors, coworkers, and fellow congregational members who are different from you.

Relationships have intrinsic value. Remember how I started chapter 2: after creating humankind, God said, "It is not good that the man should be alone."[1] God has created a world around us complete with a network of people. We will need one another to accomplish any of our goals. We will need others to help us create legal or cultural changes. And others will need us to help make the world a little more just, a little more caring, and a little more loving. Our nurturing of relationships can only help us learn, grow, accomplish our goals, refine our strategies, and redirect our energies. It is good for our individual advocacy and good for us as a society, helping one another fill others' shortcomings.

REFLECTION AND ACTION

This "Reflection and Action" section will look a little different. Spend time mapping the networks of relationships that can help advance your advocacy. Think of someone who has the power to act in a helpful way on the issue you are advocating for. We'll call this your target person: _____

1. Who does your target person listen to? This can include constituents, customers, stakeholders, and community leaders. Make this list as long as you can. If you can name specific people, that is also helpful:

   _____

   _____

   _____

2. We'll call the people you just listed "secondary influencers" to your target person. Now, list all the people the secondary influencers listen to:

   _____

   _____

   _____

Continue this chain of influence until you have mapped a connection between yourself and the target person you are trying to reach. This map helps you figure out how to start personally and build up to the influencer for your issue.

5 | KNOW YOUR AUDIENCE'S VALUES

I spent the last chapter talking about your sphere of influence within your own personal networks. Mapping relationships helps you know how you can get to the targeted decision makers by building your influence. Now, we are going to dive further into the values that motivate your target audience.

We can't influence everyone in the world, in the country, or even in our communities. But we have people who we know and, perhaps more importantly, know us. We spent the last chapter speaking about making personal connections with the people we are trying to influence through existing relationships or connections. The additional benefit is that we know what they value, what they fear, and what motivates them. We can shape our arguments to match their worldview because we understand that worldview. We can give calls to action that match their values and their skill sets because we know what they may be willing and able to do. We also know when to back off and let them have space to process or ask questions.

This will sound a little strange, but we need to shape our arguments to the values and worldviews of the people we are trying to influence. "It's just the right thing to do" doesn't work when people don't agree on what the right thing is. Our worldviews are often shaped by what messaging expert George Lakoff describes as frames.[1] These frames are the lenses through which we see and interpret the world. They incorporate our values, biases, stereotypes, and ways that we process incoming information. Lakoff reminds us that frames are strong and resilient. Facts often bounce off well-established frames. That means people don't understand a particular set of facts the same way others do. We need to make facts relevant to the frames, cultures, and values of others if we want to get them to act the ways we intend.

Go and Do Likewise: Lakoff also advocates for reporters to use the "truth sandwich."[2] When covering a known falsehood, start by stating the truth. Then briefly describe the falsehood, followed by a reiteration of the truth. Indivisible adapted the truth sandwich for advocates fighting disinformation.[3] Start by stating truthful common values. Then question the motive of the disinformation. Finally, end with a vision or call to action that builds a better future. Try the truth sandwich when talking to others.

INVOKE YOUR TARGET AUDIENCE'S VALUES

The book of Acts tells a story of how Paul used this same principle while he was visiting Athens. While in the city, Paul noticed all the statues of and altars to various Greek gods. As Acts puts it, "He was deeply distressed to see that the city was full of idols."[4] Paul studied the culture of the Athenians, a highly curious and learned society. He argued with others in the synagogue and the marketplace, the forms of media in his day. His arguing attracted a crowd that was interested to learn about something new. This eventually got him in front of the Athenian city leadership. He could have used his time in front of the city leaders to condemn and berate the Athenians for their idolatry, angering them and turning himself into a martyr. But that likely wouldn't have changed any hearts and minds. Instead, he adapted his sermon to the values and worldview of Athenian culture. First, he affirmed the religiosity of the Athenians, saying, "I see how extremely religious you are in every way."[5] He then used a specific example of their religiosity—an altar with the inscription "To an unknown god"—as a way to introduce the gospel of Christ.

Paul's sermon was as about effective as it could be. Acts says, "Some scoffed, but others said, 'We will hear you again about this.'"[6] They wanted to hear more and invited him back to keep sharing. Had he simply condemned them, he wouldn't have gained those immediate followers, nor would he have had the opportunity to continue his evangelism. He was effective at gaining followers of Christianity because he shaped his message to the worldview of his audience.

In the same way, we need to think about the audiences we are trying to reach, how they understand the world, what they value, and how we can best present information so that they will join us in our movement and do what we ask them to do.

MAKE THE ISSUE RELEVANT

In 2012, a year after I moved to New York, anti-LGBTQ activists in Minnesota succeeded in placing a marriage amendment on the state ballot. It would be one of the last proposed statewide constitutional amendments that would enshrine marriage inequality in a state. Up until that point, ballot initiatives proposing marriage amendments were used as a popular tactic for bringing conservatives to the polls and electing Republican officials, a strategy openly embraced and boasted during major election years like 2004.[7] However, the tide was changing, albeit slowly. In order to defeat this constitutional amendment, it would take as much outreach and effort as we could muster.

I knew that I needed to convince my grandmother to vote no on the referendum. I grew up with her as a regular fixture in my life. She lived in the same town that I did. I spent significant time at her home growing up. I went to her place before and after school. When I had activities early in the morning or late at night, I often slept at her place. She was like a third parent to me.

Because I knew her so well, I tailored my conversation, using her values and concerns to convince her that voting no was the right thing. She was in her eighties and widowed. As such, she had an assumption that the marriage amendment wasn't going to impact her life in any way. In her experience, being gay was associated with scandal. The thought of loving, committed same-sex couples getting married was completely off her radar.

I also knew that my grandmother loved me. She was proud of my accomplishments, seeing them as reflections of her influence in my life. She encouraged me to take up music so she could hear me play the piano or sing, either directly to her or in public.

However, she struggled to accept me being gay. My family has that Minnesota Scandinavian conflict-avoidant attitude, so there was never a direct confrontation. I waited a long time to come out to her, and she didn't want to talk about it a lot. Later, when Richard and I were early in our relationship, she was cordial but distant. At one point, she casually mentioned that perhaps I should come up and visit by myself. I didn't say anything, but my mother pulled her aside to warn her that if she continued to say things like that, I would stop coming to visit altogether, something she didn't want to happen.

In fact, she cried when I called to inform her that I got my job at GLAAD and that I was moving away from Minnesota to New York City. To her, that was far away, with even less possibility to visit. My grandma loved me a lot and wanted me to be in her life. Over time, she learned to be more comfortable with me being gay and with my relationship with Richard. I think it helped when she figured out that Richard could help fix her computer.

When it came time to ask her to vote no, I needed to make a case for why this was going to matter to her. Because we had a close relationship, I let her know that the possibility of a marriage amendment would harm me, her beloved grandson. And then I took it a step further. Remembering how she cried when I let her know I was moving from Minnesota to New York, I told her that the passage of this amendment would make it difficult or even impossible to return to Minnesota in the future, since my marriage wouldn't be recognized in the state.

Yes, that was a knife-twisting moment. I made her understand how she, an eighty-something widow, might be harmed by a constitutional amendment banning marriages between people of the same gender. I was also helping her connect her values—family, safety, and loyalty—to the needs of the moment. I helped her see how the marriage amendment would violate her values and how voting no was the best way to live them out.

KNOW THE VALUES OF YOUR TARGET AUDIENCE

Each audience is going to be different, and it is worth spending time thinking through how they express their values and their motivations. If we ask them to do something that they think violates their values or their worldview, they will resist. What we are asking is not a violation of their values but rather an extension of them. We have to make the case that the action we are asking them to do is something they believe in.

The people with whom you have influence will be motivated by different things, and their worldview might not match yours. It is worth spending time thinking about values—your own and those of the person or the community you are trying to convince. Then think about how you can shape your advocacy to the way they see and understand the world and the values they say they hold so dear.

This may sound a little cynical, and it is, but if we truly want to motivate people to take action in a particular way, we are going to have to frame the issue to match their values. The reason we start with people with whom we have a connection is that we understand what their influences are and what they truly value. It is much easier to ask people to take action as an extension, rather than a violation, of their values. The more we understand the values of our target audience, the better we can shape our arguments and our calls to action, even if we don't necessarily hold the values.

The same is true for communities and churches. What does your congregation value? While you might utter the obvious Sunday school answer of "Jesus," it's worth going further. How do people describe your congregation? What is it best known for? Some congregations want to be known as "Bible-based" churches. If that's your place, you had better have some good scriptural arguments ready when making your case to others. (We'll cover this more in depth in another chapter.)

Your congregation may be known as a good place for families, drawing in parents with children to take advantage of the programming. That means your congregation values family and will interpret most things through that lens. Perhaps your congregation values stellar worship experiences, engaging preaching, community fellowship, or service to the world. Convincing your fellow congregational members to join you in taking action, whatever form that action takes, will be much more impactful and effective when you describe it through the existing values of the congregation. People will see the action as an extension of the congregational community. They will be more likely to explore it, incorporate it into congregational activity, and ultimately, do what you ask.

DIG BELOW THE STATED VALUES

Doing an analysis of other people's values has to be done carefully and strategically, without judgment. Ask yourself what is motivating your audience under the surface. What do they fear? What do they hope for? Sometimes, people will come right out and tell you, but there's often more lurking behind the scenes. The better you know them, the more you may understand what's not being said underneath their talking points.

As a teenager, I didn't like swimming. People assumed it was because I couldn't swim or that I was afraid of the water. In reality, I was self-conscious about the scars on my back from spinal surgery. Anyone who spent energy and effort trying to teach me to swim or make me comfortable with the water was missing the real issue. Instead, they could have been much more effective by addressing my body image and self-consciousness.

Before you ask someone to take action, do a nonjudgmental review of their values. If you don't have any idea, perhaps your first step is a friendly meeting and conversation where you can learn what their values and worldview are. After you feel like you know them, you can ask how your issue and, more importantly, the action you want them to take connect with their values.

Of course, different people may value different things. In your congregation, someone might believe that small groups keep them engaged and connected to the congregation. Others may believe that a dynamic worship experience is the most important thing to them. And, of course, these disagreements may pale in relation to more "political" topics raised in the congregation. When you are speaking to an individual or a small group of people, instead of speaking in generalities, it is helpful to be as specific to the person or small group as possible. Of course, when addressing a larger group, like at a congregational meeting, you may have to invoke the values you believe apply to the most people in the room. But then, be sure to follow up with key people with tailored messages that will speak to their worldview.

This goes beyond just your congregation. Your community also has values—or things that it values. Are your fellow citizens proud of the schools in the area? Do folks brag about the town's thriving business community? Do people enjoy that "neighborliness" that the community has? All of those are values—and great frames to apply to the way you talk about the issue you are representing or how you frame the ask. They are great values to invoke as you speak in front of the city council or have a meeting with your mayor or local police. They should be incorporated in op-eds and posts on neighborhood social media platforms. They should undergird your ask to take a specific, tangible action.

Asking someone to do something that deviates from their values is incredibly hard. What you need to do is convince people that the action you are asking them to take—whether it is to vote, attend a rally, contact their representatives, or whatever—fits in with their values. As Christians, we are people who speak of values regularly, so it shouldn't be a foreign concept to us. We live our values, and we speak about them. We hold common values that bind us together in a community, whether that's our church, our town, our state, or even our country.

REFLECTION AND ACTION

Reflect: Whether thinking about a person, your congregation, or your community, what values does your target audience hold?

Reflect: How can you connect the issue you are advocating for with the values of your target audience?

Act: Write talking points that frame your issue within the values of your audience. What are the ways you can frame your issue so that your target audience understands their action as an extension, rather than a violation, of their values?

Act: Share those talking points with a fellow advocate within your community to hone and refine them to make them even more powerful.

6 | DETERMINE OPENNESS AND ACCEPTANCE

When I lead trainings for GLAAD, I sometimes ask people to tell the story of how they first became convinced that they need to be involved in their particular area of activism or why a particular issue has pushed them to action. Often, someone says, "It's just the right thing to do."

Of course I agree with them personally. They are attending a training I'm leading, so we are probably there with similar values and motivations. My job is to remind these advocates that other people don't believe that something is "just the right thing to do." In fact, in our world of misinformation, disinformation, both-sides journalism, and social media distortion, we may not even agree with others about the reality of the world around us. We cannot assume that people are motivated in the same way we are about a particular issue. Even more daunting is how willing they are to act on their agreement.

Part of knowing your audience is figuring out how easy or difficult it is going to be to motivate them into action. That can help you figure out who is willing to help with little prompting, who might take convincing, and who could end up being an obstacle.

FOCUS ON THE "MOVABLE MIDDLE"

If we laid out society in a spectrum (or even better, as a bell curve), our allied base would be on the left end. These are the folks who largely "get it" with regard to our particular issues. They are aware, and they tend to agree with us. They are likely the ones we have met with when we are working our way out of isolation and into connection. Your main goal with your allied base is to keep them energized, thank them for what they've done, and then give them the next thing to do. We can ask them to take on increasingly difficult tasks because they are already motivated.

To the right end of the spectrum is the opposition. These are the folks actively working against your advocacy. It's not impossible for them to move toward acceptance, but it will take a lot of time, energy, and attention or something traumatic happening in their lives. In many but not all cases, converting them to your position may be more trouble than it's worth.

Floating between these two extremes is what we at GLAAD call the "movable middle."[1] We describe them as good people who want to do the right thing but often are conflicted about what that right thing is. They often don't know the issues as well as advocates do, since they aren't paying attention day in and day out as we have. They likely don't look past the headline of a story, meaning they lack nuance in their understanding. They may believe whatever frame is being fed to them through their communities or the media they consume. If the media doesn't cover a story, they may not even be aware that it exists. If the media frames something as dangerous or controversial, they will believe that the issue is dangerous or controversial. This is why it's important to frame our messages and our calls to action around the values and worldview of the movable middle, whatever those might be.

The movable middle is not simply "white midwestern middle-class voters," which is often how they are framed in our culture. Think of election news coverage. A lot of media attention is spent focusing on suburban, white, middle-class voters, with much less attention paid to people of color, those living in urban or rural communities, the working class, or people living in poverty. The idea of "white midwestern middle-class voters" is an oversimplification that reflects our bias toward whiteness as the norm.

Go and Do Likewise: The Public Religion Research Institute provides polling data on American attitudes regarding a variety of issues, including reproductive health, climate change, economy, immigration, criminal justice, LGBTQ, race, religion, and sports. Its reports also provide a breakdown by a variety of factors, including religion, gender, race, and political affiliation. Use this data to shape your understanding of acceptance within your target audience.

In fact, every population and every community have an allied base, an opposition, and a movable middle. Sometimes, communities get painted as either "liberal" or "conservative," but those labels overlook the diversity of opinion that exists within a community or the mix of understandings of and approaches to different issues that don't line up with labels like "liberal" or "conservative." Take, for example, the United Church of Christ, typically considered a liberal denomination. In reality, there are extremely conservative members and entire congregations within that denomination. On the other hand, the Roman Catholic Church has been defined by conservative issues like opposition to abortion and LGBTQ people's relationships. However, Catholic support for immigration, opposition to the death penalty, and opposition to violence align with more progressive stances. The best way to think of the movable middle is to understand it as the population that the allied base and the opposition are both fighting to sway to their side.

UNDERSTAND THE NUANCES OF ACCEPTANCE

However, thinking of these three categories as separate buckets doesn't really provide enough nuance. If you think of our population as a spectrum or a bell curve, then you can see that there are movable people who are closer to allyship and others who are closer to opposition. One way I encourage people to think about it is this: How much energy and effort will it take to get the person to do what you are asking? If you were to hold a rally, the allied base would attend just because they care about the issue. The opposition would be holding a counterrally or trying to sabotage yours. Movable middle people might show up, perhaps because you invited them and they care about their relationship with you. Others might come out of curiosity, to try to learn more. Some would stay away, deeming it too controversial or radical for them. And some would attend because you made the right case to them.

Emily Eastwood, my boss at the organization now called ReconcilingWorks, used to talk about various gradations of acceptance. She was citing from a book titled *Embodiment* by James B.

Nelson.[2] Nelson wrote about sexuality and Christian theology in the late 1970s, just as the organization that became known as Lutherans Concerned, and even later as ReconcilingWorks, was being formed.

Nelson was writing about the range of what he called "theological opinion about homosexuality." The four stages he used were *rejecting-punitive, rejecting-nonpunitive, qualified acceptance,* and *full acceptance.* As he wrote about these four stages, he outlined the logic and values that undergirded each position. However, the closer I looked at Nelson's stages, the more they seemed to apply to understanding and relationships with all kinds of people, communities, and issues that were different from our own. It was a span of understanding and acceptance—and how much someone was going to engage with a particular issue.

Combining Nelson's four stages of theological opinion about homosexuality with GLAAD's focus on the "allies–movable middle–opposition" spectrum, I started to craft my own understanding of how people engage with difference and advocacy. This framework helps us think about where people are, how we can best determine where they are, and the best way to move them toward allyship.

PUNITIVE REJECTION → SILENCE → TOLERANCE → ACCEPTANCE → ADVOCACY

Punitive Rejection

Punitive rejection is just what it sounds like. This person is in active opposition. They do not accept the same principle you are advocating for. Additionally, they often want to punish people who don't conform to dominant cultural norms—usually white supremacy, patriarchy, and strongly enforced gender roles. A rejection position can be caused by a variety of factors.

Why would people maintain the punitive rejection position? There are some who hold this position so they can maintain power and control. But many of us remain in a punitive rejection mindset because we are captive to the sins of white supremacy, patriarchy, and gender roles. Cable news, social media, and yes, even the messages we hear from the pulpit often promote conflict based on difference. The intention is to reinforce the fear of difference, using that fear to tolerate or, worse, foment violence against those who are not straight white men. Christianity has also violently upheld those same cultural norms through the empire of Christendom. Biblical interpretation, preaching, and church polity in the West have given patriarchy and white supremacy a veneer of religious significance.

Punitive rejection can take many forms. Bills, laws, and policies that criminalize, control, or censor race, gender, sexual orientation, ability, or any form of difference are written and passed in a spirit of punitive rejection. Some examples include bans on teaching about race, racism, slavery, or LGBTQ identity. Other examples include informal policing of hairstyles, clothing, or language that isn't deemed "professional" because it aligns with a minority identity. Bullying, harassment, or disapproving comments can also fall under the punitive rejection frame of mind.

Silence

Here's the thing about someone who is in punitive rejection: the person in this stage is actively and vocally opposing your work. Just getting them to shut up is a win. This is moving someone from punitive rejection into silence. The Indivisible founders said some lawmakers may silently oppose an action or a bill without drawing attention to their opposition.[3] They stop adding to the debate around an issue, just wishing it would go away. In a world saturated with hot takes and propaganda, this silence can be helpful.

But we don't want people to stay in silence. Silence isn't a change in mindset but a grasp of the consequences of saying opposing sentiments out loud. This is the person who still holds bigoted beliefs but knows they will be scolded for saying them out loud. People in the silence stage know slurs have consequences but fear the consequences for themselves more than the harm such slurs might cause others. The silence stage may make it easier for you to advocate for your issue without having to constantly combat the opposition, but it doesn't do much to change hearts and minds.

Tolerance

We hope we can move people beyond silence into the next stage: tolerance. A person in the tolerance stage is learning to understand and accept that God's diversity is bigger and grander than their limited worldview. They may not be comfortable with difference, but they have learned to be nice and cordial . . . to tolerate. It is, at most, a recognition of the people and issues that exist beyond their immediate experience.

The advantage of tolerance is the ability to live and work together, giving people the opportunity to learn from others and expand their worldview. It opens the possibility of growth through relationship building. The drawback of tolerance is there won't be an immediate benefit. The door is still open to misunderstanding, lack of awareness, and microaggressions. Tolerance rarely moves people to action, and our goal is to motivate people to act.

Acceptance

We want to move people to the acceptance stage, building real, human relationships with folks to listen and build understanding. When people are in a true relationship with those who are different, they are more likely to take action in moments of distress, hardship, or discrimination, with some prompting. They might speak up because someone they know and love may be harmed by the current circumstances.

The difficulty with acceptance is that it can still be stymied by a lack of initiative and the threat of complacency. Some-one may take action when prompted or when the situation is dire enough, but often people rely on their lack of overt punitive action to keep them from having to do more. People who quickly claim the title of "ally" can fall within the acceptance phase, with little follow-up or long-term action. Remember the black squares posted on Instagram after the police murder of George Floyd? People shared them with the intention they would be a sign of solidarity, but they had the consequence of drowning out Black voices who were trying to share information and create a strategy to respond to ongoing police brutality. Once the moment passed, support for the Black Lives Matter movement dropped.[4] Racism and violence against Black Americans continued beyond that moment, but many people in the acceptance stage didn't remain active. We need people to be proactive and consistent in their actions. Acceptance can help us get there, but people can go even further.

Advocacy

The final stage in my continuum is advocacy. This is a proactive stage, stepping up to do what needs to be done without having to be convinced or even asked. It is understanding the issue enough to know what you know, what you don't know, and that you feel compelled to do something about it. Advocacy is a hard stage to maintain because it takes the most self-reflection, correction, and change in strategic action. It is keeping up with changing news and strategies. It requires knowing when to speak up and when to keep silent. It means being immersed in and committed to an issue or a community, even when you aren't impacted directly. This is the moment where you may believe that "it's just the right thing to do."

FOCUS ON STAGE-BY-STAGE PROGRESS

These are all stages that can apply to any particular issue. The strategies you use to move someone from punitive rejection are different from what you would use to move someone from tolerance to acceptance. You might be able to silence an opponent with social stigma for their point of view, which changes the words, images, and ideologies they are putting out into the world, but it doesn't change their heart or their worldview.

Understanding what stage people, organizations, or communities are in can help you plan how you approach them, what you can feasibly ask them to do, and what might motivate them to act.

People can't leapfrog over stages. It is not realistic to expect someone to go from punitive rejection to advocacy—at least, not with our feeble human capacity. A traumatic event, however, could make them rethink their whole worldview. Think, for example, of a parent learning simultaneously that their child was queer and also the victim of a hate crime. While learning about the crime, they might suddenly realize how their words and actions may have impacted the child they love so much. These sorts of traumatic moments create a "road to Damascus" effect. Near the start of the book of Acts, Saul had been violently persecuting Christians until he saw a blinding light, was thrown off his horse, was blinded, and heard the voice of Jesus speaking to his heart, directly challenging his actions.

Even after his experience on the road to Damascus, Saul needed others to take him in, teach him, and guide him into an entirely different worldview. Ananias laid his hands on Saul to proclaim the message of Jesus. Once Saul regained his sight (and changed his name to Paul), he still needed to be fed, led, and taught. "For several days he was with the disciples in Damascus," according to the book of Acts.[5] The time Paul spent with the disciples was likely needed to answer his questions, address his concerns, and shift his worldview. Even while Paul "immediately . . . began to proclaim Jesus in the synagogues, saying, 'He is the Son of God,'" he was learning, growing, and likely progressing through each of the stages of acceptance.[6] And this is all at a much more rapid rate than we can likely expect for ourselves and our actions.

A few things to remember about this spectrum: First, just like people can progress, they can also regress through the stages. Personal experiences can strongly alter someone's worldview, and sadly, fear is very effective at moving people back toward the punitive rejection phase. Trauma can send us in both directions on the spectrum, depending on its nature and our interpretation of it. We could be scared back into distrusting others, or we can be compelled into understanding the struggles of others even better.

Second, no one is in the same stage of acceptance for every single issue. Just because someone is accepting of or advocating for LGBTQ issues, doesn't mean they will be in the same stages regarding racism. This is why labels like "liberal" or "conservative" are overly simplistic. They attempt to summarize complex issues into a single word. Understand that you may have vocal active support on one particular issue but experience silence or tolerance on something else.

This is all part of better knowing your target audience. Your target can be a person or an organization. While we individually hold any of these positions, organizations often formalize them into policies and culture. Think carefully about the issue you are working on and the realistic reaction your target has to that issue. Use their words and actions as guides, and reassess if you see movement in a particular direction. Celebrate the movement forward, but always recognize that there is often much more to do and further to go.

REFLECTION AND ACTION

Reflect: Think carefully and critically about your target audiences. They can be people or organizations.

Act: Place each of your target people or organizations along the spectrum of acceptance, listing some reasons why you believe they might be placed there. You cannot know for certain what is in their hearts and their minds, but you can take an educated guess based on what you know about them. Write down what you know about their values, their fears, and the sources they trust for information. This will help you prepare a plan for how to reach them effectively.

Punitive Rejection → Silence → Tolerance → Acceptance → Advocacy

Act: If someone is already in the advocacy stage, congratulations! This is someone who is primed to help you with your cause. If they aren't already in your core group, invite them in and get working!

7 | THINK BOTH SHORT TERM AND LONG TERM

One of the challenges of advocacy is that we must react to urgent, immediate harm while also trying to build a better future. Exclusively working toward a better future ignores a lot of present suffering and can result in irreparable damage. But dealing with crises can feel like a game of *Whac-A-Mole*, where we can't improve things because we are just trying to stop the current hurt.

When I was working for ReconcilingWorks, the way we talked about our worldview was "full participation in the life of the Lutheran Church." That is a big, lofty worldview-type goal. But what makes "full participation"? The very notion can be exemplified by dozens, even hundreds of different policies and experiences. We had to focus on a tangible outcome. In the Evangelical Lutheran Church in America (ELCA), there was a specific policy document—called *Vision and Expectations: Ordained Ministers in the Evangelical Lutheran Church in America*—that had been used as the basis for punishing and preventing LGBTQ clergy and their relationships. The policy included a line that said, "Ordained ministers who are homosexual in their self-understanding are expected to abstain from homosexual sexual relationships."[1] That sentence became a point of enforcement and discipline for LGBTQ people in the denomination.

That policy, effectively banning LGBTQ clergy in same-gender relationships, was a specific, tangible obstacle to achieving full participation in the life of the Lutheran Church. It also had a direct impact on so many people who had been defrocked and removed from church leadership, denied advancement in the process to become clergy, and discouraged others with gifts for ministry from ever applying in the first place. Of course, it was not the only obstacle to full participation: there were long-held scriptural interpretations, societal attitudes about the nature of LGBTQ people, and a repressive culture that discouraged people from examining and talking about sexual ethics. Those issues are essential, long term, and a bit more amorphous.

After years of protests and complaints about *Vision and Expectations*, the ELCA embarked on a study process on human sexuality and potentially recommend changes to the document. So ReconcilingWorks embarked on a campaign to revise or remove that particular line. The study process was intended to take four years, but it stretched into eight. It might be hard to think of how an eight-year campaign is considered short term, but the reality is that we were working on one very narrow, specific policy that would impact only a portion of the population; it was nowhere near the worldview of full participation.

After eight years of working individually, congregationally, and denominationally, in 2009, the ELCA voted to recognize and allow clergy to be in same-gender relationships. While those who opposed LGBTQ inclusion in the church tried to claim the ELCA was opening the floodgates to every form of sex, sexuality, and relationship, the scope of the policy change was narrow, a slight opening of the door. The language employed was "life-long, monogamous, same-gender relationships."[2] Queer chosen family, polyamory, parenting, sexual health and education, and much, much more were not included in the revised version of *Vision and Expectations*. Marriage wasn't even explicitly included but only hinted at (in 2009, marriage equality was far from a uniform national reality in the United States). Many LGBTQ advocates noted that the document still took a traditionally heteronormative approach to dating, relationships, and marriage. Transgender people were not protected or even included at any significant level in the policy.

Even with all those shortcomings, we celebrated it as a win. It was a milestone, one that we hoped would build momentum to the next milestone, and the next, leading us ever closer to the vision of full participation in the life of the ELCA and setting a precedent that other mainline Protestant denominations would follow.

But the hardest thing for momentum is a major win. An eight-year campaign is a long time. It consumes your attention and energy. For the hundreds of people volunteering to make this change, the 2009 decision was the payoff they had been looking for over the course of the last eight years. They were tired, and they wanted to take a break or focus on other essential areas of advocacy.

Meanwhile, the opposition, those who were opposing the policy change, spread the message that the sky was falling. There were angry congregational meetings where opponents tried to pull congregational memberships out of the ELCA. What was a modest step forward for us was a slippery slope for them.

We immediately went from celebrating this milestone to fighting about its implementation and the backlash it caused. What was forgotten in all this? Our long-term goal: full participation in the life of the Lutheran Church. It was something we talked about as an organization, but for many, the milestone was the short-term policy win. Some asked if we were going to close down now that we had won. Funders who supported us through the fight for the policy change backed off, redirecting their efforts to other worthy causes. Volunteers who had given more than eight years of their lives refocused their energy and attention elsewhere.

We had missed an opportunity to frame this as a milestone in service of a larger vision. That larger vision can't only be mentioned at the end of a campaign but rather needs to be incorporated into a specific initiative's messaging. Yes, we need this milestone, and we will work for it, but it is always in service of the larger vision of full participation in the life of the Lutheran Church.

THINK BEYOND ONE ELECTION CYCLE

When we are advocating for something, we need to help people see the big picture, and then we need to outline how the immediate action we are taking today leads to that big picture. We don't want the short-term win to harm the momentum toward the big-picture goal; rather, we want it to be a milestone along the journey.

Our public political and election advocacy works in the same way. We want to see action on the issues important to us: policies to address climate change, budgets that protect our social infrastructure, laws that allow people to support themselves and their families. Elections are just about choosing the people we believe are most likely to enact those laws and policies. We focus a lot on elections, but they themselves don't bring about the actions we really desire. Winning them doesn't immediately enact the legal and policy changes we seek. There is still a process of passing a bill through the legislature or issuing an executive order. Putting people in office who are more likely to pass policies that line up with our goals and values is an essential first step to getting our preferred laws and policies enacted. Even after electoral wins, though, we will need to ensure the people we elected act on our issues.

It's very frustrating when we work hard to elect leaders who don't go on to enact laws and policies that protect humankind, reduce inequality, and secure a future for everyone. So part of the follow-up after elections is to communicate to your elected leaders that you expect them to pass laws and create policies that you want. But it is harder, of course, to get the policies we seek passed when our elected leaders are opposed to our goals and values.

Go and Do Likewise: Even though elections are short term, democracy is a long-term goal. Voting rights and access to the ballot are essential for every eligible American citizen. Check out what voting rights and restrictions exist in your state. Join forces with the many organizations fighting for voting rights, registering voters, protecting access to the ballot box, and ensuring our democracy lasts for the long term. You will find several organizations at the end of the book.

Elections are not onetime events; they're not even every-four-years events. They are constant and cyclical. There are many elections every year, from general elections and primaries to runoff elections and special elections. In the United States, we have a range of officeholders, from the president down to specific local offices like the school board, city council, library board, and so much more. All these officials have the opportunity to support or oppose your work. While they get less media attention, local offices have a more direct impact on our day-to-day lives than federal offices. Think of the control the local school board has over the curriculum, bullying, student organizations, and the hiring and firing of teachers. The same dynamic plays out in parks and recreation boards, county commissioners, and city governments. That's why it's important to focus on local elections. You want allies—people who agree with your values and are working to enact the policies you seek—at the national, state, *and* local levels. If you don't have elected leaders who line up with your values, then you should consider running for one of those local offices in order to enact immediate change and build momentum for working on these issues at higher levels.

I say all this to put elections into perspective. The election is an important step, but it cannot be the victory. The victory comes when we have laws that protect people. And we have many opportunities and methods for impacting both immediate and long-term change.

BUILD THE FUTURE WE WANT TO SEE

As religious people, we should be very good at understanding the bigger vision. Our Scripture is cosmic and apocalyptic, attempting to describe a God who is both bigger than our creation and so intimate to know us better than we know ourselves. We have stories, songs, and prayers that imagine life when sin and sorrow are no more. We let people see the kingdom of God through the lens of the actions we are taking today. We believe in an abundant future that is possible while recognizing what the reality is around us. This vision is tied into our confession and absolution of sin, our reading and interpretation of Scripture, and our prayers. We can recognize so many ways that our world doesn't function the way it should, but we also believe in a God who has the power to create a world that is very good. We recognize that the milestone is essential while reminding people that it is not enough to achieve the larger vision. We apply a theological lens to what is happening in our world, putting the news into the perspective of God's creation, Christ's redemption of the world, and the Holy Spirit's continued advocacy among all of us. This theology isn't necessary to act for justice, but it can be a guide for those of us who are Christian.

We can also look at the countless examples of people who have seen immediate needs in the world and worked to build long-term solutions. One good example is DaShawn Usher, my colleague at GLAAD. DaShawn balances his day job at GLAAD advocating for the fair, accurate, and inclusive representation of the LGBTQ community with his powerful community-organizing work for queer Black people, as well as working toward the eradication of HIV. All of these are major, audacious goals. Any one of the goals is overwhelming, unlikely to be fully achieved in our lifetime.

In addition to his work at GLAAD, DaShawn is also the founder and executive director of Mobilizing Our Brothers Initiative (MOBI). MOBI is a community-centered initiative that focuses primarily on health and wellness for the Black LGBTQ community. Its programming focuses on "curated social connectivity events for Black gay men and queer people of color to see their holistic self while promoting community, wellness, and personal development."[3] Embedded in MOBI programming and events are opportunities for community-based organizations to share resources, party planners to promote cultural events, entrepreneurs to highlight their businesses, specialty experts to provide education, and community to drive conversation meant to empower the Black queer community.

I asked DaShawn why he started MOBI, and he took me through a bit of his personal history. He had been working for HIV organizations doing both clinical research and direct service work with youth. The long-term work was research, continuing to find effective treatments, cures, and prevention for HIV. His short-term work in direct services helped people living with HIV get resources for medical care, housing, and so on.

DaShawn started out doing HIV clinical trials and "youth outreach"—he laughed. "Youth. My peers." He told me about attending the Conference on Retroviruses and Opportunistic Infections, related to his HIV work. At that conference, researchers shared data that said that one in two Black gay men have a lifetime risk of contracting HIV. DaShawn said, "I thought, 'Wow. That should not be the case.' But there weren't many other people in the room who looked like me, and no one else flinched or was outraged. Most people responded, 'Yeah, that tracks.' After learning about that, I felt a call to action to want to do something 'in the now.'"

DaShawn discovered that traditional health and wellness work for Black LGBTQ+ communities tends to only center on HIV and sexual health and does not see this particular community holistically. This limited view of what the Black community should prioritize healthwise does not address the other social determinants of health. In fact, there often is a lack of funding to address other critical life issues this community faces, including housing insecurities, professional development, unemployment or underemployment, nutrition, and mental health.

Getting help and treatment for people living with HIV is an immediate task. Eradicating HIV is a long-term clinical goal. But building a strong community that focuses on holistic wellness, access to resources, and self-determination for one's future is a multifaceted, long-term, worldview-changing goal. DaShawn found he had to do all of the above. It started by identifying the problem: queer people of color weren't able to access the resources available. He said, "So many people were coming into our trials who didn't know about any of the HIV-serving organizations available to them. They were aware of the larger, more popular organizations and clinics, but those often had a long waiting list. It was frustrating because they didn't know about clinics and resources that were right in their own neighborhood." That was the impetus for MOBI. The idea was that through events, conversations, and cultural initiatives, Black queer men would build resilience, access resources, and build a better, safer future for themselves.

DaShawn also learned that conferences weren't the only answer: "I volunteered with a national group called Young Black Gay Men Leadership Initiative. We'd put on these summits for young Black gay men. People would come to the summits with appreciation and community and then go back home to a hostile world." Through his ongoing partnerships with larger organizations, he realized that with his own organization, he could identify and promote the right resources for Black gay men and queer people of color. MOBI understands the richness of the Black LGBTQ+

community and the subset communities that are often ignored. It creates original programming to be a bridge of information and resource sharing while working to build personal well-being and stronger community connections that shift the narratives of the Black queer community.

Even while he is meeting immediate needs, DaShawn is building for a long-term future. Through MOBI's community activations, GLAAD's advocacy work, and his own personal passions, he is reminding people what the future could be like.

VISUALIZE THE FUTURE YOU WANT TO SEE

What can we learn from the example of DaShawn's work at MOBI? When you are starting to engage in advocacy around an issue, let yourself visualize what the world would be like when you achieve your vision. What would be in that future? What would *not* be in that future? What would people be able to do that they cannot do now? What would look different from the world we live in today?

As you examine your vision, start to write down the concrete, tangible changes that need to come about to make that larger vision a reality. Those are your milestones, your markers that you are getting ever closer to the vision. Next, think through what would need to happen to achieve those milestones.

This also helps you organize your energy and efforts. Which milestone will you focus on? Perhaps the one that has momentum behind it or that you can collaborate on with others who have been doing this work for a long time. There were gay and lesbian people criticizing and protesting the exclusive policy within the ELCA for years, but the opportunity came when the study process was announced. Now we had a specific target, with the clearest opportunity to change the policy.

Remember, just as you choose a certain milestone to focus on, other people and organizations will focus their energy on other milestones. It's always helpful to stay abreast of what others are doing, finding points of mutual collaboration but also respecting the distinct approaches that others are taking.

Keep in mind that achieving the short-term milestone is not the fulfillment of the vision. We want to celebrate each achievement along the way, but we always point people to where the vision lies and the next thing to accomplish. You might join forces with a person or group who has been working on another aspect of your issue.

The important thing is to keep the big worldview goal in the front of your mind, in your messages to others, and in the way you craft your strategy. Your big worldview goal might exist beyond your effort or even your life. This is when we remind ourselves of the cosmic nature of the advocacy we are doing. God's vision goes further than ours. We can then resonate with the apostle Paul, who wrote to the church at Corinth, "I planted, Apollos watered, but God gave the growth."[4]

REFLECTION AND ACTION

Reflect: What is your worldview around the area of advocacy you are focusing on?

Act: Write it down in a single sentence.

Reflect: What tangible signs would signal that you've achieved your worldview?

What wouldn't exist that exists today?

What would exist that doesn't exist today?

Act: Share your worldview with others in a variety of settings. Share it not just with people who agree with you but with those who are in the silence, tolerance, or advocacy stages. Take note of their reaction.

Reflect: What milestones need to be achieved in order to make this worldview a reality?

Act: Choose one milestone, the one that will build the most momentum, and start working on how you can achieve it.

8 | USE SCRIPTURE

Finally, we are at that fun chapter that I've been waiting for! This rule seems pretty easy. It could be summed up in the title: use Scripture.

One of the biggest accusations against progressive Christians is that we've "thrown the Bible out the window" when we advocate for LGBTQ people in the church, racial justice, fair wages, or any other progressive issue. As Christians, our silence on the Bible works against us. There are plenty of people asserting that there is a "clear scriptural message" that dictates what issues we should focus on and what positions we should take on them. That interpretation is informed by a worldview that upholds white supremacy and patriarchy, allowing those in power to control the interpretation.

Of course, Scripture is most often used in arguments against LGBTQ people, abortion, and more "sexual" topics. We hear Scripture cited so much less frequently by conservative figures on the matters of economic justice, preserving the environment, climate change, immigration, and dismantling racism. And yet those topics show up in Scripture, often quite explicitly. The fact that they are ignored is all the more reason for you to invoke them, especially with others who claim Christianity for themselves. Later in this chapter, we'll cover a quick starter list of

Scripture that could support progressive causes. First, we need to get a better background on the role of Scripture in our advocacy.

One major problem is that so many of us are intimidated by our inability to quote or cite Scripture by chapter and verse. We constantly hear others throwing around single verses that seem to match up with their messages. It is intimidating. How do they just know the magic verse that goes with what they are saying? We can't do that, so we opt to not say anything at all.

I will confess to you, here and now, that I am a seminary-trained deacon in the church. I have read the Bible multiple times, and I cannot cite the chapters and verses of most passages, with perhaps the exception of verses that were made into songs, but only then if the song included the passage citation, like "Ephesians 4:32" (if you know this song, you are probably singing "Ba dum bum!" right now).

But my years of reading and studying Scripture have given me the ability to tell Bible stories in a way that connects what the biblical characters were facing to our lives today. I use the language and imagery of Scripture in conversation, painting a picture of how it influences my thought process. That doesn't fit on a bumper sticker, but it does influence how I live my life.

I think a lot of us fear that not being able to cite every possible passage of Scripture means we shouldn't engage at all. Another barrier is that many progressives don't like the way conservatives have used "Bible bullets," little bits of proof texting, plucking out single verses without any larger context of Scripture. We don't want to use a singular verse pulled out of context to make our point.

The challenge for us as Christians is to not repeat the same harmful practice from a progressive standpoint. Scripture is a source that informs our faith. It describes an ongoing relationship between God and all of creation. It's complex, contradictory at times, and filled with content that makes us ponder. I want us to get more comfortable doing the long-form Bible study that has informed our faith for centuries, applying it to the issues and topics that we care about, alongside the ability to share a tangible, memorable sound bite of Scripture that can stay in someone's head and inform them on what God might be calling us to do in a particular issue.

USE BIBLE STUDY AS A FOUNDATION OF YOUR ADVOCACY

In your preparation to engage in a particular issue, spend time in Bible study. Look up the stories, the psalms, the prophets, and the laments that may have themes that speak to the issues you are advocating for. Look for your issue in unexpected places. You might find inspiration in a story that seems to be completely unrelated. Think of Jesus's two questions to his disciples in the book of Matthew—"Who do people say that the Son of Man is?" and "Who do you say that I am?"[1]—and ask yourself how often you've asked your closest friends what other people may be saying about you and then been vulnerable enough to ask for direct feedback on your life and work. The minute details of who is mentioned, what specific actions were taken, or the form of the wording can provide some context of what God's will might be for our world.

Go beyond explicit mentions in the Bible. You won't find *carbon-neutral* or *minimum wage* mentioned. Most of what governs our lives in 2023 isn't in the Bible: the internet, 401(k)s, multinational corporations, capitalism, the United States. However, the themes of economic justice are there. Calls for human dignity for immigrants, widows, orphans, and the poor all appear. Stories of oppression and solidarity with the marginalized show up, which we can apply to our everyday lives.

GET COMFORTABLE WITH SCRIPTURE

I think, for the good of our ministry, we need to think of Scripture as a reflective text. We should see ourselves in biblical stories, poems, prophecies, characters, and emotions. If we cannot relate to any character, any emotion, any event in Scripture, then it's not relevant to our lives. And if that's the case, then the Bible is an old book of stories about other people in a land far away, thousands of years ago—one that has nothing to say about our lives and our world today.

The reality is, though, that we *do* see ourselves in these stories, and that's why we find them relatable. Even when we read stories of miracles and supernatural events, there is something very human and very tangible going on in them.

I once preached on Jesus walking on water. While I was preaching, I kept emphasizing that the reaction of the disciples was completely understandable and relatable. And then I confessed that I didn't relate to Jesus in that story. In it, Jesus knew what was going on. Jesus knew they would all be safe. I can't relate to that. I sure can relate to the disciples in the situation. I don't know what's going on. I don't know that we are going to be safe at any given moment.

That's the kind of way we can look at Scripture and apply it to our lives today. We can find ourselves thinking and feeling the same thing as the disciples, or the prophets, or King David, or even Jesus was in a given moment: anger and frustration, joy and dance. We know what it feels like to be grappling with the same issues that we see coming up in the Bible.

If you are still feeling overwhelmed by Scripture, then I have an exercise you can try. Take a sheet of paper, and fill it with your most meaningful passages of Scripture. If you know them, you can write the chapters and verses. Or you can write out the passages word for word. Or you can summarize them. Or you can give them titles ("The story of the Good Samaritan," for example). Choose those passages that give you life, that have personal significance to you.

Maybe some of the passages come from particularly meaningful moments in your life. They might have been read at a baptism or funeral, and they always remind you of that person and your relationship together. Whatever the connection, keep brainstorming those passages, and write them down in one place. Don't stop until you've filled the page.

Once you have the page filled, take a look at what you have written. You know Scripture better than you realize. You are aware of the stories and themes. It has never been about citing a chapter and verse. Those numbers were not in any of the original documents but inserted years later. What is more important is the messages. And you know them; you just filled a page with them.

These passages are connected to your advocacy because they are connected to your values. They make you who you are, and they should inform your advocacy in the wider world. If nothing else, you have these passages to fall back on when you are talking about justice and love and equality. Your already existing knowledge and love of Scripture can also drive you further to examine what it might have to say about the issues you are working on. Use your existing base as a way to examine what else the Bible might be saying to us in our time.

> **Go and Do Likewise:** Develop a thirty-second elevator pitch that connects your issue to Scripture. Something like, "I support climate justice because Psalm 24 tells us that the earth and all that is in it belongs to the Lord." What elevator pitch can you come up with?

START WITH THESE ADVOCACY-RELATED SCRIPTURAL SUGGESTIONS

This is not an exhaustive list, and you should really do your own research to find the passages that resonate the most with you, but I'm going to give you a rapid-fire list of Scripture passages that just might inform your progressive values. You can cite these in your conversations with fellow advocates, your congregation, people in power, and your friends and family. I need to follow my own rule about avoiding Bible bullets and providing fuller context, and I encourage you to read the stories around these passages so you can more fully understand their contexts:

- ♦ When discussing a fair minimum wage, you can always repeat Jesus's words in Luke 10:7: "The laborer deserves to be paid." Heck, you can even cite the same words a second time, as when 1 Timothy 5:18 repeats the sentiment.

- ♦ When calling for a universal basic income that sustains life, you can remind people of the story Jesus told about the day laborers who were all paid the same wage despite starting their work at different times. When some workers complained, Jesus reminded them that God's generosity is poured out upon many, and it is not about who was hired first or worked the most (Matt 20:1–16).

♦ When advocating for an immigration policy that treats refugees, asylum seekers, and migrants with dignity and respect, you can remind people that Abraham left his homeland to enter another just because God told him to (Gen 12:1–4). Later, Abraham lived as an alien in Egypt in order to survive a famine (Gen 12:10). You can also mention that the Holy Family has something in common with today's refugees and asylum seekers, having to flee to a different land out of fear of violence and persecution (Matt 2:13–23). The story of the baby Jesus, Mary, and Joseph should be repeated alongside the stories of pregnant women and mothers who come to the United States fleeing warlords, gang violence, or a government that persecutes them, just like Herod was persecuting his perceived threat: a newborn baby.

♦ When talking about the risks involved with coming out as a part of the LGBTQ community, you can compare the LGBTQ coming-out experience with that of Esther, who had to weigh the dangers of coming out as Jewish before a king who had criminalized Jewish people. When reading this story of a beloved queen with a secret about her own identity, people may better understand the decision-making process that happens when a person decides to come out.

♦ We have come to know Joseph's "coat of many colors" in Genesis 37, but the Hebrew name for the garment, *ketonet passim*, is only used in one other place in the Bible: 2 Samuel 13:18. It is worn by Tamar, the daughter of King David. It is described as a garment specifically for a king's daughters. Is it possible that Joseph was wearing a "princess dress" instead of a "coat of many colors"? Does that change the brothers' reaction? Does that impact the story later, when the brothers are reunited with a grown-up Joseph whom they can't even recognize?

♦ David and Jonathan are often labeled as "special friends," but is it possible they had a torrid affair? The first time Jonathan laid eyes on David, he stripped in front of him and made a covenant. That is a good example of love at first sight (1 Sam 18:1–4). As you continue to read 1 and 2 Samuel, you see affection, kissing, crying, and pledges of devotion between the two men.

♦ Speaking of love and fidelity, the pledge so often recited at weddings—"Where you go, I will go; where you lodge, I will lodge; your people shall be my people and your God my God"—was originally a promise between two women (Ruth 1:16). Naomi made this pledge to her mother-in-law out of both love and commitment, knowing that they were stronger together than separate.

♦ Anti-racist and anti-xenophobic examples are found throughout Scripture, starting with God's creation of all people in God's own image. They continue with figures like Moses, who married a woman of a different race and respected his father-in-law as an authority figure

(Exod 18); the Good Samaritan (Luke 10:25–37); Philip, who conversed with and baptized an Ethiopian eunuch (Acts 8:26–40); and Paul, who pushed the early church to look outside its self-imposed boundaries (Gal 2:11–14). The book of Acts is filled with stories of Christianity expanding its membership beyond "the chosen people" to include those who had been explicitly excluded.

♦ When advocating for decriminalizing and destigmatizing sex work, you can cite Matthew 21:31 to remind people that Jesus told us sex workers will enter the kingdom of God ahead of religious leaders. Jesus said this to the religious leaders who confronted him to demand by whose authority he was doing his ministry. In fact, there are many sex workers in the Bible. They are never condemned but often helpful to the biblical heroes.

♦ The book of Numbers provides a formula for how to perform an abortion (Num 5:11–28). Granted, it's for a man suspecting his wife of infidelity, but it has some pretty explicit instructions on how to do it.

♦ There are a lot of economic commandments concerning the well-being and treatment of the poor and those who are economically vulnerable. Perhaps the most explicit directive is when Jesus tells a young man, "Sell your possessions, and give the money to the poor," followed by, "It is easier for a camel to go through the eye of a needle than for someone who is rich to enter the kingdom of God" (Matt 19:16–24).

♦ This list would not be complete without referencing the Magnificat, Mary's prophecy about how God was turning the world upside down, scattering "the proud in the imagination of their hearts," filling the hungry with good things, and sending the rich away empty (Luke 1:46–55). Mary's song flies in the face of the prosperity gospel, which signifies wealth as a sign of God's blessing.

This is just a starter list, and not every passage will fit every situation. You can find so many more progressive values, stories, and themes among the pages of Scripture if you approach it with the right lens and a mind open to read what God has to say. That's why, as Christians, Scripture is important to us, but we have to be willing to truly dig in and engage with the text rather than relying on others to do our interpretations for us.

INCORPORATE SCRIPTURE INTO YOUR MESSAGES

The final step is to incorporate Scripture into your messages. Do not let a conversation go without including your most life-giving Bible verse on your desired topic. Practice having them ready so you can seamlessly incorporate them in conversation, testimony, and written pleas for a more just world. Write Scripture passages on signs to bring to rallies and protests. Add them to your social media posts. Cite them when calling up your elected official to urge them to vote for or against something. Bring them up in Bible study, sermons, or teaching at your church.

In short, use Scripture. It is there to provide guidance, comfort, agitation, and a sense that we are created and called by God to do this work on earth. It should be for your own spiritual grounding but also to inform and enhance your advocacy.

REFLECTION AND ACTION

Reflect: What are the Scripture passages that give you life?

Act: Write a list of your most life-giving passages of Scripture. Include notes about what themes of love and justice they invoke.

Reflect: How are these passages of Scripture connected to the advocacy you are doing?

Act: Every time you talk about your issue of advocacy, use one of your passages of Scripture. Verbally make the connection between the Bible and the issue you are advocating for.

9 | FOCUS ON IMPACT OVER MOTIVATION

So much of what we've talked about so far has been focused on the target audience (the *who*) and what we want them to do (the *what*). The *why* is the hardest part of the question. It's much harder to think about why someone might want to do something. What is their motivation? And even worse, what if their motivation is different from mine? Can those things reconcile?

I've mentioned this before, but it's worth bringing up here again. When I ask people why they support LGBTQ inclusion in the church or in society (or a host of other progressive causes), they often come back with "It's just the right thing to do."

And often, I personally agree. I think it's the right thing to do too, which is why I'm working on these causes. But there are lots of folks who do not recognize our advocacy as the right thing to do. They might be in a punitive rejection stage or part of the opposition, claiming that the right thing to do is the opposite of what we are advocating for. However, most people may not have dedicated any mental energy to thinking in any depth about our issues or causes. They may not care all that much.

To be honest, most people are focused on their own lives and the things that impact them most. In our media-saturated world, they may not know more than some basic headlines or talking points. The things that are discussed in the news often seem very far away from their lives. And our media doesn't make it any easier. News sources frequently frame politics as something that happens elsewhere, in Washington, DC, or in state capitols. Conflict is nearly always overseas, in remote lands thousands of miles away from the routine of our everyday lives.

And there is *so much* news. So much, we don't ever hear about all the things that are happening. Our media picks and chooses what stories it covers and which ones will get ignored.

I had a meeting with a producer from a news program in 2014. I was sharing a resource we had created at GLAAD. When I asked if he would include some of the ideas in an upcoming show, he paused and said, "I don't know if we'll be able to. We are pretty much all Ebola, all the time." While I recognized that the Ebola outbreak was one of the biggest news stories of the time, I also learned that the strategy of this particular outlet was to focus on one story to the exclusion of everything else happening in the world, with talking heads that examined, reexamined, pontificated, and debated their main story over and over.

What a news outlet chooses to include and exclude from coverage shapes the reality of its consumers. An outlet doesn't have to be intentionally nefarious with its coverage, but by telling certain stories and ignoring others, it creates a perception of what is a crisis and what is not urgent. In New York City, where I live, despite crime being at historically low levels, people believe it is skyrocketing. Why? Because New York City crime gets more media attention, locally and nationally, than other stories.[1]

With an information flow like this, is it any wonder that most people haven't given much thought to the causes we care so much about? They truly have no opportunity to learn even the basics about some of these issues until we can find a way to reach them.

FOCUS ON CONCRETE ACTIONS OVER MOTIVATION

Are these folks lost causes because they haven't thought about our issues in depth? Do we just ignore them? Absolutely not. In order to make a real impact and lasting change, we need to engage those folks who might act—if we can give them a reason to do so and make it compelling and worth their while to take the action we need.

We cannot know what is in their hearts and their heads with any level of certainty. This is a pesky, frustrating fact that we just can't ignore. There remains the real possibility that people will do the right thing for the wrong reason. One of my bosses once said to me, "We can't make people do the right things for the right reasons. We just need them to do the right thing, but we can't control the reasons why they do it."

That insight has sat with me since it was uttered. It reminds me of a parable Jesus tells in the book of Luke:

> In a certain city there was a judge who neither feared God nor had respect for people. In that city there was a widow who kept coming to him and saying, "Grant me justice against my opponent." For a while he refused; but later he said to himself, "Though I have no fear of God and no respect for anyone, yet because this widow keeps bothering me, I will grant her justice, so that she may not wear me out by continually coming." And the Lord said, "Listen to what the unjust judge says. And will not God grant justice

to his chosen ones who cry to him day and night? Will he delay long in helping them? I tell you, he will quickly grant justice to them. And yet, when the Son of Man comes, will he find faith on earth?"[2]

Notice that the judge in the parable never has a conversion moment. His heart never melts. He doesn't become a "good" person. He still doesn't fear God, and he still doesn't respect people. Instead, he is tired and worn down. The widow's persistence has made *not* acting in the right way painful for him. He grants justice, albeit begrudgingly.

The judge's action is the right thing (granting justice) but for the wrong reason (to stop the annoyance). So what's the impact? What good does that do? For the widow, it probably does quite a bit. We don't know how she was wronged, but it was enough that she was motivated to be persistent. And she got her justice! She won. It wasn't pretty, but she got there. From the widow's perspective, it doesn't matter what reasoning the judge used. The impact of his action was what she was advocating for.

BE PRESENT AND PERSISTENT

We've seen this similar strategy in contemporary advocacy.

In 2013, the North Carolina legislature enacted a series of regressive laws and policies, including cutting unemployment benefits, refusing federal funding to expand Medicaid, and enacting a voter ID law that specifically targeted Black Americans. In response, people of faith began showing up at the North Carolina General Assembly building in a protest that came to be known as Moral Mondays. That protest movement saw throngs of protesters under a different theme each week. One week, the focus was on reproductive rights; another week, on criminal justice reform.[3]

The leader of Moral Mondays was Rev. William Barber, a local NAACP president. Since Moral Mondays began in 2013, Rev. Barber has become a ubiquitous presence, calling out injustice that harms Americans and using biblical language. Through Rev. Barber's work, Moral Mondays shifted into a revival of Rev. Dr. Martin Luther King's Poor People's Campaign.[4] Like Moral Mondays, the Poor People's Campaign is multifaceted, advocating for several issues that disproportionately impact marginalized voices.

Included among the list of principles for the Poor People's Campaign is a need for continued direct action "as a way to break through the tweets and shift the moral narrative."[5] Moral Mondays demonstrators showed up at the North Carolina General Assembly every single week, calling for justice for women, people of color, unemployed people, immigrants, LGBTQ people, victims of gun violence, and so many more. Hundreds of participants, mostly religious people, were arrested for civil disobedience. They stood on the assembly grounds, ignoring calls from authorities to disperse. The then North Carolina governor Pat McCrory was not swayed by the protesters' actions. He would ignore, dismiss, or disparage the group, first claiming they were outsiders, then calling the crowd "disrespectful."[6]

However, the Moral Mondays demonstrators continued to show up, just like the widow in Jesus's parable. Even if the governor and state assembly would not listen to their cries for justice, the movement was still getting media attention, reaching the voters of North Carolina. After the voters consistently heard from Rev. Barber and the Moral Mondays movement for a couple of years, they voted to replace Governor McCrory with Roy Cooper.

Of course, the struggle continues. North Carolina is a purple state, and change continues to take persistence. Rev. Barber and the Poor People's Campaign continue to show up and speak out. They consistently use biblical and moral language to describe their work and their vision for a just society.

What can we learn from Moral Mondays and the Poor People's Campaign? That showing up consistently, with a unified message, works. Despite the wide range of issues addressed by the Poor People's Campaign, they are tied together with a consistent overarching message. Consistency is really the key. Of course, it's hard for one person to be consistent. We have ever-changing daily demands that mean we can't always show up at every rally. That is why working with a larger organization is helpful. When you can't show up, others will.

MAKE YOUR ELECTED LEADERS KNOW WHAT YOU STAND FOR

Let's look at another example of an organization that uses persistence. Remember Indivisible from chapter 2? I gave a brief introduction, but we'll dive into their strategy here. Indivisible was formed after the 2016 election. A married couple, both former legislative staffers, wrote a manifesto that spoke of the need to be persistent in calling for justice, preventing bad legislation, and possibly pushing for positive legislation. As legislative staffers, they had lived through the Tea Party movement, fielding daily calls, visits, and rallies from constituents affiliated with the Tea Party pushing for or against particular action based on the movement's anti-tax, anti-government principles. They argued that progressives needed to adopt these tactics to protect democracy in the United States. Eventually, their manifesto spawned an organization with chapters all over the country employing the tactics with their local, state, and national leaders. The couple wrote a book, drawing from the manifesto and the successes of the organization's chapters on important items like preventing the complete repeal of the Affordable Care Act in 2017.[7]

In both the document and the book, the authors advocate for the same strategy as the widow against the unjust judge. They claim that any elected leader's primary motivation is reelection. Every statement and action is evaluated through the lens of whether it will help reelection prospects. Perhaps an action is popular with constituents, earning their goodwill. Perhaps it will please a donor who will write them a big check. Perhaps it gets them positive media attention, so their constituents can see them doing something. All these lead to reelection.

It is as cynical as the judge in Jesus's parable. But it means that you might treat the elected leader as if they "have no fear of God and no respect for anyone."

Knowing that motivation helps craft how we engage. Boiled down, the strategy involves continuously staying in contact with your elected leader, constantly pushing them to do more, publicly challenging them when they go against your wishes, and publicly thanking them when they do the right thing. They may not be moved by your morals, ethics, or values. They may be moved if you consistently remind them of your presence and your values as you publicly criticize, call for better action, give them bad media attention, or praise actions that align with your values.

Go and Do Likewise: Enter each of your elected leader's contact info into your phone to make dialing and emailing quicker. You can include your US senator, state legislators, governor, mayor, and even city council members. If they have multiple offices, enter all the phone numbers. Sometimes, during pressing issues, voice mails fill up, and you can call an alternative number. Having the contacts in your phone will make your outreach much easier to do.

Indivisible recommends being persistent, although not abusive. They advise calling your elected leaders every day. Calling is more effective than social media or even sending auto-generated emails. Staffers keep a tally of what issues people are calling about and what side they are advocating for. They often check to see if you are a constituent because constituent voices have more influence. On the call, tell the staffer what you want the elected leader to do. Most often it will be voting for or against legislation.

If you have enough time, an even more effective tactic is visiting your elected leader's office. You may only be able to talk to a staffer, but you can continue to convey your concerns. In some instances, if you have an elected leader who is adamantly opposed to justice or the stance you are taking, they may refuse to see you. If so, then document your visit, including the fact that the elected leader refused to see you. Let their other constituents and the media know that they are ignoring calls for justice from their own constituents.

Indivisible encourages you to show up at every town hall, every open house, every public appearance where they will be just so they know your presence. If you can, ask them questions or urge them to support or oppose legislation.

Online petitions, auto-generated form emails that all look the same, and social media criticism are all less effective options. If legislative staffers get multiple emails that say exactly the same thing or a single statement with hundreds of names at the bottom, they will count it as one contact. On the other hand, each call and handwritten letter, even from the same person, will be counted individually. The contacts that take more time and attention will be more impactful than something that requires a couple of clicks on a webpage.

Let's be clear, if your elected leader is opposed to the position you are taking, you are probably not going to change their mind. But you should still call, visit, and show up at their events. You should still make your positions known, along with the actions you want them to take. Like the unjust judge in Jesus's parable, sometimes elected leaders change their position because it's what their constituents want. Sometimes they will move from punitive rejection to silence, not supporting the opposition so vocally. Sometimes they may change their position just to make the calls and visits stop! We need to recognize both of these as a win, a milestone in the spectrum of acceptance.

REMAIN PERSISTENT WHEN YOU GET A RESPONSE

Indivisible cautions you against settling for the first answer you get. When you bring an issue to an elected leader, they will likely respond in a way that looks or sounds like they agree with you and your position, even if they are in stark opposition. You speak of violence against LGBTQ people, and they respond, "No one should face discrimination." That's a great sentiment, but it has no impact. What action are they taking? Part of the persistence of the widow is to return with your clear call for a specific action.

This doesn't only have to apply to elected leaders. The same is true for businesses that are hurting the community but have good marketing that can cover whatever wrongdoing they are committing. It's true for incalcitrant religious leaders whose actions aren't lining up with their beliefs. It's true for anyone in power, no matter what form that power takes.

Your persistence has to be strategic. You have to know what you are trying to get them to do and what the best way is to get them to do that specific thing. Sometimes your strategy is going to involve a protest or rally. Other times it will be speaking to the media. At yet other times it will be direct outreach and behind-the-scenes negotiation. Persistence is even more effective if it's targeted and focused on the person you are trying to move.

The biggest takeaway from this parable is not to simply take no for an answer, especially from high-profile public figures whose actions will have a major impact on your community. I've heard too many people say that their elected leader is a "lost cause." Instead of giving up on them, take a lesson from the widow in our story. Return, and continue to ask for (or even demand) what you need. You can visit, write letters, call, or show up at their public appearances. If they won't talk to you, then talk to your community about their actions: write an op-ed, write a letter to the editor, or create a social media campaign that invites others to reach out to the elected leader.

An important part of this is also praising the leader when they do the right thing. That positive reinforcement works especially well when paired with criticism. Then, let them know you'll be in touch about the next important thing you need them to do.

But don't give up. Your elected leader may not fear God or respect humans, but they do respond to ongoing pressure. And by continuing the pressure in the name of love and justice, you are doing God's work.

REFLECTION AND ACTION

Reflect: Identify a leader you are trying to convince to take a particular action. The action may be a vote for or against a piece of legislation. Think of their motivations, especially their desire to stay in power. What can you do to reach them to convince them to do the action you want?

Act: Plan to contact your elected leader on a regular basis:

- Call the office.
- Write a letter or postcard.
- Visit the office.
- Attend public events where they will be.
- Email them.
- Respond to them on social media.
- _____
- _____
- _____

Reflect: How can you cultivate attention around your elected leader's action or lack of action and invite others to join you in reaching out to them?

- Op-eds or letters to the editor
- Billboards
- Sandwich signs
- Rallies
- _____
- _____
- _____

Act: Start with one item on the above list. Writing a letter to the editor may be the easiest place to start, but something else might be a better fit for you. While direct contact with the elected official should be regular, these wider actions can be occasional. So start with one.

10 | GET CREATIVE

In 2007, in the midst of the campaign to compel the Evangelical Lutheran Church in America (ELCA) to adopt policies of greater LGBTQ inclusion in the life of the church, a visible symbol showed up at the ELCA Churchwide Assembly: the rainbow scarf.

We were still two years away from adopting a social statement on human sexuality or a policy change to allow LGBTQ clergy in same-gender relationships, but this Churchwide Assembly was a significant step in the process. The rainbow scarf became the symbol for the movement of welcome and inclusion. But where did it come from?

Months before, Lutherans Concerned was leading an ecumenical training on faith-based community organizing at a Unitarian Universalist church. The hosts wore knitted and crocheted scarves made out of rainbow variegated yarn so people knew who to approach for directions and logistical questions. They were intended to be visible symbols of hospitality.[1]

Emily Eastwood, the executive director of Lutherans Concerned, admired the scarves, saying they would be helpful at the upcoming Churchwide Assembly. The Unitarian hosts said that they would make some, asking Emily how many she might need. After pondering for a moment, Emily responded by asking for five hundred. The Unitarian ladies took deep breaths and said they could do it. When Emily told Jerry Vagts, the grassroots organizing coordinator, he thought that some knitting and crocheting Lutherans might want to make their own scarves. He sent out an email asking others to make some. The directions included basic parameters but allowed for creative freedom. The scarves were to be of certain dimensions and made with variegated rainbow yarn. After that, people could knit or crochet in any pattern they wished.

That email was quickly passed around to others, people who had been looking for something to do with their idle hands and anxiety about the upcoming votes on LGBTQ people in the life of the church. By the time the Churchwide Assembly began, that initial request for five hundred blossomed into over two thousand. I was one of the volunteers at the assembly opening package after package filled with scarves, piling them on a table in the middle of the volunteer room. Because we had so many, distribution wasn't limited to leaders or active volunteers. Anyone who wanted a scarf could wear the symbol of LGBTQ inclusion and acceptance in the life of the church. The scarves, when they weren't wrapped around the neck, also looked like short stoles, another reminder that we were fighting for LGBTQ clergy in same-gender relationships to be allowed to serve the church. In its reporting, the *New York Times* included a large color picture of pro-LGBTQ Lutherans in their scarves.[2]

The campaign was so successful, we attempted something even bigger two years later. Instead of scarves, we asked people to knit or crochet prayer shawls. The idea was to have both a visible symbol and an aid to support people's devotional practices. Once again, we gave the dimensions. The shawls were bigger than the scarves, so each one took longer. We asked them to make the shawls one solid color rather than a rainbow. The idea, Emily told me, was that together we form a rainbow. Again, crafters could use whatever pattern they wished. We didn't get as many—only a few hundred rather than thousands. However, the shawls proved just as popular, which was helped by the fact that the meeting hall was freezing cold, and people used the shawls to stay warm!

BE LIKE JESUS! GET CREATIVE.

When we are thinking of advocacy, some actions have become tried and true. Calls, letters, and visits with elected and community leaders allow personal engagement. Rallies and protests gather the masses to create momentum and capture a media moment. Petitions demonstrate the power behind a movement and build your list of contacts who you can call on to help with future actions. Op-eds and letters to the editor reach your neighbors with your messages. Social media posts can provide moments of dopamine but don't always land with their target audience.

But you have so many more ways to get your messages out there, and this is where you can harness creative energy—your own or others'. The scarves and prayer shawls activated people's creativity and gave them a task to do when they weren't able to be physically present.

Challenge yourself to think of other creative ways you can get attention and empathy for your issue. Musicians, artists, actors, and playwrights have long found ways to incorporate advocacy into their craft. You can do the same thing with quilting, woodworking, ceramics, pottery, or whatever your craft of choice is.

Go and Do Likewise: Create a pop-up artistic display that features your network's advocacy. This can be as simple as using your church's lawn to stage a performance for the people who walk by. If your church is by a busy road, think about a large-scale banner or sculpture that quickly captures attention and makes drivers think about the issue.

One group that has been excelling at this is the Center for Artistic Activism.[3] For years, they have worked with advocacy groups to encourage and facilitate the natural creativity we have to solve the problems we are facing. I first became aware of the organization when it led a workshop during a retreat on ensuring a fair taxation system and economic justice across our state. The founders, Stephen Duncombe and Steve Lambert, have also written a book, *The Art of Activism: Your All-Purpose Guide to Making the Impossible Possible*.[4] The book is filled with multiple examples of creative forms of activism but also warns that we cannot completely replicate one tactic in another context.

One of the leaders whom Duncombe and Lambert hold up to emulate is none other than Jesus Christ. They are very clear that they are looking at his tactics rather than his divinity, but he is a model of how to do advocacy in a creative manner. Of course, as Christians, we get to draw encouragement and inspiration from both Jesus's divinity and his creative actions during his earthly ministry.

The authors focus on several examples of when Jesus employed creative activism. First, instead of handing down principles or statements of values, Jesus told stories. His parables were confusing and left up to the listeners (or the readers, hundreds of years later) to interpret. That was intentional. "Unlike a list of grievances or demands, easily understood and just as easily ignored, the parables asked listeners to puzzle through their mysteries and meanings. . . . And with every argument and counter-argument they made, Jesus's words ceased to be his alone," Duncombe and Lambert explain. "Through interpretation, his teachings became the common property of his audience and cemented their belief."[5]

They note that Jesus's miracles were also a form of creative expression, tapping into the popular media of the day. Many in Jesus's time would perform miracles in order to gain a following, but Jesus reserved his miracles for the benefit of the poor, sick, and marginalized. When urged to use a miracle to benefit himself, by both Satan in the wilderness and the crowd witnessing his crucifixion, Jesus declined. His miracles were not for his personal gain but for ensuring that good news was able to reach those who were downtrodden.[6]

If you are reading this book, I assume you believe in the divinity of Jesus more than the leaders of the Center for Artistic Activism, but their point is incredibly well taken. Jesus used media, creatively performing miracles, to proclaim the kingdom of God and to call attention to those whom society ignored.

In the hundreds of years since Jesus walked the earth, we have continued that artistic tradition. Music has enhanced our worship, architecture has designed beautiful church buildings, and we fill those buildings with artwork, but we don't often apply that same artistic expression to our faithful advocacy. Our churches are likely already filled with artistic people who care about important issues but don't know how they can get involved.

Imagine asking your choir to sing a hymn about the beauty of God's creation at a rally for protecting the environment. If you wanted to go a step further, the choir could sing an original piece written for the occasion. It could perform a parody of an existing, well-known song with the words changed to get your point across even further. Then you might film a video of the song, sharing it across social media, making the performance and the message go viral and get shared beyond your local community.

What are other ways that you can creatively call attention to the problems of this world? You could line up or stack pairs of children's shoes in a prominent location on your lawn or church property to represent children who are victims of human trafficking or being bullied for their race, ability, sexual orientation, gender identity, or anything else that implies difference. You could create sand sculptures that call attention to climate change and the drying conditions in the American West. You can dress in the costumes of the Gilded Age elite to call attention to income inequality, perhaps offering to take some of those "old-timey" photos for passersby. Of course, the photos should include information about the inequality we face today, reminding participants that the Gilded Age is not over.

The only limits are your own creative imagination!

FIND WAYS TO STICK IN PEOPLE'S MINDS

The important thing is to find something that will stick in people's minds: a visual image, an experience, a logo, or a catchphrase. After a jury acquitted Trayvon Martin's murderer, Alisha Garza wrote on Facebook, "Black people. I love you. I love us. Our lives matter." Patrisse Cullors modified that sentiment into

#BlackLivesMatter, which became a chant, hashtag, and entire movement. Garza, Cullors, and other Black Lives Matter leaders enlisted a creative agency to design a logo that continues to be recognizable to this day.[7] Closely related is the image of a raised fist—both an action and a logo to represent defiance. Over the years, the fist has been used to demonstrate resistance against oppression but has also been coopted by white supremacist movements.[8] The rainbow flag, designed by Gilbert Baker in the 1970s, became an iconic representation of a whole community. Even as I write this, I see images with the blue and yellow of Ukraine's flag and artistry including sunflowers. All of these are artistic choices that stick in our collective memories and communicate something even bigger than the images themselves.

Another book that's been informative to my advocacy has been *Blueprint for Revolution: How to Use Rice Pudding, LEGO Men, and Other Nonviolent Techniques to Galvanize Communities, Overthrow Dictators, or Simply Change the World.*[9] The author, Srđa Popović, lived through a Serbian dictatorship, finding ways to hasten the overthrow of Serbian dictator Slobodan Milosevic. His circumstances may seem much more extreme than those that we'd face in our communities, but there is much to learn, no matter how big or small our struggle for justice is. In *Blueprint for Revolution,* Popović dedicates a whole chapter to humor in protest. Think about how you can make people laugh and participate. Anger at injustice may be motivating, but humor can make the oppressive opposition seem less omnipotent, reducing them to real, everyday people who can look just as stupid as we do.

I was no fan of the Tea Party, but those people knew how to work a theme. I remember seeing images of people wearing wide-brimmed hats with tea bags hanging down like Minnie

Pearl's price tag. It looked dumb, but that was the point. That mental image has stuck in my head more than a decade later. T-shirts are easy to get printed, but people will really remember those creative outfits that capture attention and are connected back to the main point of the advocacy.

Think back to the work of Conie Borchardt from chapter 2. Her advocacy work is community building and trauma healing, accomplished through song, storytelling, and art. She is vulnerable enough to share herself through her creative skills, and she encourages others to do so through Biracial and Rural, Freeing Refrains, and the other initiatives she's built. Her work is interpersonal but powerful for building a community that can be resilient in the face of trauma and also feel supported enough to change the world for the better. All that is happening because Conie encourages people to use art and song when words fail. When words are available, they can be channeled into storytelling.

Similarly, the people who make memes for sharing across social media have found a way to channel artistry into advocacy. These graphics convey simple messages with powerful visual images. Some are funny; some are poignant. The difference is the intentionality that is put behind them. The more they are shared, the more progressive values are instilled in people's heads.

I don't want you to abandon the tried-and-true methods of contacting your representatives, writing op-eds, attending rallies, and voting. None of the leaders I've mentioned in this chapter believe creative activism is a replacement for those methods. Creativity enhances our core advocacy work, grabbing more attention, sticking in people's minds, and frankly, making activism more interesting and fun.

REFLECTION AND ACTION

Your toolbox for advocacy should be growing. There is no one way to get your message across, and there are a variety of gifts that are needed. Brainstorm some of the most outlandish, creative ways you can call attention to your issue. For now, do not consider restrictions on resources like money, time, and people.

Reflect: If you had all the resources in the world, how could you creatively address the issues we are facing? This is a brainstorm, so write every outlandish idea you can fathom.

Act: Now that you have some wild ideas, start to think of what ones might work or how they might be adapted with the resources you have available.

Act: Where might you get the resources you need to accomplish any of these campaigns? Reach out to your network to share your idea and see if they have ways to contribute to or enhance it.

11 | WORK IN COALITION, BUT BE AUTHENTICALLY YOURSELF

In 2012, Minnesota lawmakers put a referendum on the ballot seeking to enshrine a ban on marriage equality in the state constitution. Prior to this, every state with a similar referendum had passed the constitutional amendment.

Quickly, LGBTQ organizations met to formulate a plan to attempt to defeat the referendum, knowing they faced an uphill battle. They formed Minnesotans United for All Families, the official campaign to defeat the amendment, backed by what theologian David Booth called "a surprising coalition of business leaders; politicians of every ideological stripe; religious leaders from many different faith traditions; veterans who said they had not put themselves in harm's way so as to shrink the range of American freedoms; armies of volunteers at phone banks; seas of orange and blue yard signs."[1]

Take a look at the diversity of that list. Organizations and businesses that may not seem directly impacted by the marriage amendment came together to vociferously oppose enshrining marriage discrimination in the Minnesota state constitution.

Since this is a book about faith, I want us to take a closer look at one part of Booth's list—namely, "religious leaders from many different faith traditions." Minnesotans United intentionally sought and organized as many different faith leaders as they could. They ended up including over one hundred faith communities and over six hundred faith leaders as a part of the faith-based coalition. These communities organized themselves by phone banking, door knocking, and visiting with fellow congregants of their own faith. Lutherans reached out to Lutherans, Muslims to Muslims, Sikhs to Sikhs, Evangelicals to Evangelicals, and so on.

These groups all signed onto the larger goal: to defeat a discriminatory constitutional amendment that would deny stability and support to a class of people and their relationships. How they went about doing their work reflected the culture and knowledge of each particular religion or denomination.

Since the marriage equality ban was being heavily promoted by the Roman Catholic hierarchy, LGBTQ-affirming Catholics formed Catholics for Marriage Equality, challenging the assumption that all Catholics would support the amendment. They published essays and op-eds using Catholic teaching, canon law, and popular Catholic vernacular to make the Catholic case for marriage equality. Those who didn't have the gift or desire for theological writing posted signs in their yards reading, "Another Catholic Voting NO." Those signs became visible witnesses to neighbors and passing motorists—any of whom might be Catholic—that perhaps the faithful choice might be to oppose the amendment. They even got a few priests wearing their priestly garments to denounce the marriage amendment.

The beauty of the coalition, even just within the faith realm, was that each group was aligned on the mission but allowed to retain their individual culture, language, and theology. Ideally, this is what working in coalition will be like. Using the same tactics over and over again can get tiresome and decrease our effectiveness. Other groups, coming from different cultures and communities, can give a fresh perspective and innovative ways to try to accomplish our goals.

Go and Do Likewise: There are many faith-based and secular coalitions that do coordinated advocacy on a variety of issues. Several national organizations and coalitions are listed at the back of this book. You can also research what statewide organizations and coalitions are in your area and might be working on the same issues you are. Sign up for their newsletters, donate to their work, and join them on a campaign that intersects with your area of interest.

UNIFY THE VISION, DIVERSIFY THE TACTICS

Some in a coalition might share the same goals and values but employ different tactics. Sometimes, a coalition will need to include radicals who are ready to flip the tables like Jesus in conjunction with skilled negotiators who can meet with leaders and ˙ opposition to chart a path forward. The goals are aligned, even when the tactics are different.

I find these complementary approaches incredibly important because I am a pretty conflict-avoidant person. I appreciate— in fact, I need—confrontational people who are ready to take to the streets, rallying, marching, and crying out for justice. If I am in a position to negotiate or be in direct contact with someone who is in the punitive rejection state, I often remind them that people are angry and speaking out. I tell them that I want to find a solution, and they can deal with me, or they can deal with the protesters who are keeping the pressure on.

We get more accomplished when we work together. This is true not just for individuals, as I discussed earlier in the book, but also for groups and organizations. Once you have your mission, a goal, and a network of people working with you, you can start to reach out to other organizations that may have a different focus but offer the opportunity to collaborate.

Working with others doesn't mean we have to lose our individual values or culture. When we work with other faith groups, we should use the language that is the truest and most authentic for our faith and identity, and we should expect and encourage other faiths and identities to employ the language and values that resonate strongest for them. We don't need to resort to generic "people of faith" language; rather, we can speak of the specificity of our faith and allow others to do the same. We don't need to bring them into alignment with our language, messaging, and tactics. They need to reach their target audience, just as we need to reach ours. And we reach our target audience when we do it as authentically as possible.

It also doesn't mean we need to merge into one movement and adopt the same mission. We are better when we have different organizations, with different cultures and different strategies. The sins of this world are legion and complex, often wrapped up against one another, and they are going to need a variety of actions to unravel them.

I've found that I work best in coalition on a project-by-project basis. When approached to help support a cause that isn't my focus area of expertise, I ask myself, "What can I contribute?

How can my participation help advance all of us? What is the best way for me to support this movement from my position?"

These questions can help you keep your focus and play to your strengths while also supporting other progressive movements. Sometimes, it is as simple as promoting the work of another organization. When you do so, you are giving them your endorsement. Your friends and followers who trust you will extend that trust to the organizations you promote. They may care deeply about this other issue and find a way to use their time, talent, and energy. You also build a reciprocal relationship where the other organizations will promote your work too.

Sometimes, you will need to build out large, formal campaigns, complete with coalitions, like Minnesotans United for All Families did. However, you can build more ad hoc coalitions as well; here's an example.

FIND OUT WHO ELSE IS IMPACTED BY AN ISSUE

Ad hoc coalition building starts with thinking through who else is impacted by the issue you are working on. During my work at GLAAD, a fellow advocate contacted me about StudentsFirst, an "educational reform" organization that had gotten significant media attention and political clout by complaining about the state of public education. The organization gained prominence with the documentary *Waiting for Superman*, which rocketed the group's founder, Michelle Rhee, to fame. StudentsFirst, however, laid the blame at the feet of teachers and their unions, ignoring inequalities driven by inequitable school funding and systemic disparities created by racism and other factors. Its primary activities were expanding charter schools, removing tenure for teachers, and weakening unions, claiming these actions would support students. Teachers unions had long recognized that this group was undermining their efforts to educate our students.[2]

This was an issue I cared about. After all, I come from a family of teachers, so I'm aware of how hard they work despite increasing class sizes and fewer resources. But GLAAD is an LGBTQ media advocacy organization, not a teachers union. What could we do?

As it turns out, StudentsFirst named Tennessee State Rep. John Ragan an "education reformer of the year." The organization also called him a "leading advocate for change." Rep. Ragan was a cosponsor of Tennessee's infamous Don't Say Gay bill, which would have forbidden teachers and school staff to talk about human sexuality in any way outside of describing reproductive function. Teachers would not be allowed to acknowledge that LGBTQ people, including their own students, existed. A later version of the bill added a mandated outing clause, requiring teachers to report LGBTQ students to their parents as well as send them to a psychologist.

That award provided a tangible reason to work in coalition. It allowed GLAAD to lead with its LGBTQ focus, while teachers unions and other public education advocates could work on strengthening their unions, reducing classroom size, improving educational standards, or other areas of focus. We were a national LGBTQ organization wading into a fight about safe, fair, and equitable education, finding the LGBTQ angle of the issue. I used GLAAD's platform to bring attention to the fact that StudentsFirst was honoring a politician who was persecuting LGBTQ students.

We were put in contact with an eleven-year-old named Marcel Neergaard, who had been bullied so severely, his parents pulled him out of school midyear to homeschool him. I worked with Marcel and his parents to build a campaign. The family launched a petition on MoveOn's website calling on StudentsFirst to rescind Ragan's honor of "education reformer of the year." Additionally, Marcel, with help from his parents and me, penned an op-ed in the *Huffington Post* describing the bullying he experienced.[3] (As a side note, when doing advocacy with children and youth, the involvement of parents is going to be an important consideration. In most cases, parents need to be willing and active parts of the campaign. At a minimum, have a serious conversation about what positive and negative implications there are for public advocacy.)

In the op-ed, Marcel let readers know that he and his family were Rep. Ragan's constituents. This opened the door for additional partners to add their voices and their advocacy from the political realm.

Within three days, the petition garnered over fifty thousand signatures, and StudentsFirst responded to the growing media pressure. They stated they stood with Marcel and LGBTQ students. They would rescind the award from Rep. Ragan and begin to support anti-bullying legislation, a position the organization had avoided previously.

CONTINUE COALITION WORK WHEN THE MOMENT IS OVER

In essence, Marcel "won." He got the specific thing he asked for. But that action didn't end LGBTQ bullying. Marcel continued to speak out against LGBTQ bullying. He joined GLAAD's Spirit Day campaign, filming videos to encourage others to take a stand against bullying. His story was told by Melissa Harris-Perry, who dubbed him "foot soldier of the week" on her MSNBC show, as well as on Nickelodeon's *Nick News*. Marcel even attended the GLAAD Media Awards, where he received a full two-minute standing ovation for his work, with celebrities and powerful media executives lined up to speak to him at the closing reception.

Marcel's case was an authentic way to work in coalition without any of us losing our identity or mission. His campaign against a Don't Say Gay bill was in 2013, but in the years since, we have seen a continued fight over education, classroom curriculum, and inclusion for marginalized students. Nine years later, Florida passed into law its own version of a Don't Say Gay law, and Tennessee is considering reviving an even more extreme version of the same bill.[4] Opposition to curriculum and texts that include people of color or LGBTQ people continues to dominate our public discourse. Demands on teachers have grown, especially as we live through the coronavirus pandemic. There are myriad ways to improve access to quality education and just as many focus areas: racism, funding, support for teachers, bullying, LGBTQ inclusion, and so on.

Of course, Marcel has grown up. He's no longer an eleven-year-old but a young adult. StudentsFirst and Rep. Ragan are no longer the key players, but new ones have popped up. The fight over ensuring quality education for all students continues, and it needs new activists, new organizations, and new areas of focus. There are plenty of places to jump in and add your particular voice or focus area.

Our continued collaboration also protects us against the forces that keep us from working together through a "divide and conquer" strategy. It is tempting to think of justice as a zero-sum game where an advance for one community is a setback in another. We must resist the whispers of that temptation, knowing that God has created everyone and everything and cares deeply about each of the issues that we face together.

So even if your focus is on LGBTQ youth, know that students of color, immigrants, and students with disabilities face their own barriers and attacks, often from the same sources. You can often find common threads running through more specialized advocacy campaigns. Joining forces with other organizations—participating in and promoting their work—only strengthens your own work.

REFLECTION AND ACTION

Reflect: Identify other communities that are also impacted by the same issue you are advocating for, perhaps in a different way.

Act: Use a piece of paper to map out the overlapping communities and issues. This can be accomplished through a list or another, more creative way to express the relationships between communities and the issues we face.

Reflect: Identify the advocacy organizations for those other communities.

Act: Reach out to build a relationship of collaboration around the problem or issue. Offer to work together or support their efforts:

♦ Amplify one another's messages on social media.

♦ Collaborate on a joint campaign or public statement.

♦ Refer volunteers, donors, and media to one another.

♦ Conduct regular check-ins to monitor recent developments and progress.

12 | PLAY NICELY WITH OTHERS

In the last chapter, I extolled the benefits of working in coalition with others, finding partners, and working together toward a common vision. I probably made it sound like it was heaven on earth, with people and organizations living in symbiotic harmony. But as you well know, we live in a broken, sinful world. Even if our intentions are worthy, we can still participate in conflict, and even harm, in our quest to do good in the world.

The reality is that every person and organization has different strategies, priorities, and values. These differences mean we will run up against one another and disagree on tactics, messages, or participation. White supremacy, patriarchy, xenophobia, and ableism can influence the planning and execution of our strategy, keeping others from being a part of the solution or benefiting from our actions.

In addition, we have a desire to have our work recognized and valued, which can lead to territorialism in which we actively work to ensure others don't receive credit for what we consider "our" work. I warn you about this so you can do the self-examination to keep those temptations at bay for yourself and also recognize when it's coming from other parties.

NAVIGATE MOVEMENT POLITICS WITH CARE

A younger GLAAD staff person came to me concerned about an email she received. She was profiling the leader of an LGBTQ religious organization, helping to get some media attention to their work. The email she received was from a different LGBTQ religious organization complaining that they weren't getting the same level of media attention or promotion from us. I said, "It's time we talk about what I call 'movement politics.'" I had to explain to her that resources like media attention and funding can be scarce, leaving each organization to feel like they have to fight for each morsel. That feeling of scarcity can lead us to hyperfocus on the good of our organization, our strategy, and our issues at the expense of others.

Of course, it should be different, but that doesn't mean it is. The book of Mark recounts a story where Jesus confronts his disciples about their infighting.[1] While walking along the road, the disciples argue over who is the greatest. Jesus uses a child to remind them that the greatest in the kingdom of heaven is the smallest and most vulnerable. This story shows how old the urge to rank ourselves against others is. It is a human urge, one that pulls us away from sacrifice for the neighbor and toward self-preservation and aggrandizement.

If any of us think that we would have acted better than the disciples in this story, think again. Even those of us who live and work in the church or in social justice movements fall into this trap. Our worthy causes are no protection from our corrupt motivations and actions. We are human, and we remain petty, searching for recognition and validation of our work, finding ourselves working against allies who act in different ways than our own.

I have that midwestern "aw shucks" demeanor, and I know that I spend a good chunk of my days working on justice and equity issues, but I want to be liked and respected. I want my work to be recognized and celebrated. I want others to be motivated to join me in the causes that I think are important. I sometimes run into conflicts with others who are also working for equality and justice and can treat them like competition instead of allies in a common cause. I remember being jealous of the red equal sign that became ubiquitous during the Supreme Court hearings and ruling that struck down Proposition 8 and paved the way to marriage equality.[2] The graphic came from another organization. Instead of recognizing the power of a creative, visual symbol, I was bitter we didn't come up with the idea.

BEWARE OF THE SINS OF NOBLE ADVOCACY

It's not just about disagreements with similar organizations. There will inevitably be times when our focus on our cause is going to lead us to do something that is not helpful or is even actively harmful to others. This is where our biases, our privileges, and the systemic nature of injustice will rear their ugly heads. We may believe that we are acting in the best interest of our advocacy, but we learn that our actions have inflicted pain and suffering on others.

If we are blessed, someone will let us know the harm we are causing. It won't feel like a blessing in that moment. It will hurt our egos to be told that our attempt to promote a particular form of justice is causing inadvertent or even direct harm. But this is guidance and correction we will need to hear.

> **Go and Do Likewise:** We need to learn from the people and organizations that are doing advocacy from a different perspective from us—socially, demographically, or culturally. Find and follow organizations that don't approach the issue the same way you do. Listen and learn how their perspective can help you advocate with an intersectional lens. Subscribe, become members, and donate to their work.

As a white, male, gay, cisgender, educated, able-bodied US citizen, I strive to be keenly aware of when my dominant privilege makes me susceptible to causing harm, even inadvertent harm, by my words, actions, and inactions. We often think about how the world works from our perspective, and the assumptions we make may not be true for others, especially when we are part of a dominant, majority population. It takes extra diligence not to re-create the same oppressive structures under the guise of a social justice mission. We will want to be carefully attuned to the impact of our actions, asking ourselves, "Who is our action intended to help?" "Who might be harmed by our actions?" and "Who might be ignored by our actions?"

We will also need to take very seriously the critiques that come from others, especially from marginalized groups. We might not get those critiques directly, meaning we need to listen carefully for hints or secondhand reports. Critiques may not be worded nicely or even constructively, meaning we will have to do the work to understand the harm and rectify it. But it is essential to see what our impact is on others, to learn how we can adjust our strategy, or if we need to shift our mission, to both advance justice and minimize harm. Maybe it means we give the decision-making control to others who are better attuned to the needs of marginalized communities while continuing to offer our help and support.

BE READY FOR JESUS TO INTERRUPT OUR SELF-CONCERN

What is important for us to remember is that God's justice—and God's love, and God's will, and God's grace—is always going to surpass our feeble human understanding. That means our way of perceiving the world, our strategy on how to accomplish things, or even our idea of what is "acceptable" advocacy may not be the only or even the correct way. Grace allows us to learn from our mistakes, confess the harm we caused, make reparations with our neighbors, and do better.

That will require us to step back from our egos to take correction and change our course of action. Because sin continues to be pervasive, our natural instinct when criticized is defensiveness. We find our work important, and when it's attacked, we aggrandize our efforts or our intention. It's a human quality, and we can act just like Jesus's disciples when they argued along the road.

When that happens, Jesus asks us the same gotcha question he asked of his own disciples: What were you arguing about on the way?[3]

With questions like that, Jesus interrupts our spiraling concerns about ourselves and our work in the world to remind us that the greatest of all is really the least of all. Jesus used a child to remind his disciples (and us) that serving Jesus means taking the needs of the most marginalized as our primary lens through which we view our advocacy. It's a disruption to our way of thinking, of processing and understanding the world.

Of course, unlike the disciples in this story, we know how far Jesus will go in his sacrifice, how he will be arrested, tortured, and executed by the power of the government. And we have a story about how he rose from the dead after three days. We may not fully understand it, but we have an idea that this is something God can do.

We should be able to take comfort in this. It means that the fate of the world doesn't completely rest on our shoulders. It means that our flawed strategy or our corrupted motivation isn't going to ruin God's plan for the world. It means that God is in control and we are not.

What do we do when we know we are not in control? The same thing we do when we learn that our strategy is causing harm. We say thank you for the correction, learn from it, and adjust our strategy according to the feedback. We recognize that we don't know everything, and we keep ourselves aware of what we don't know. We look to the people who can fill in the gaps in our action and knowledge.

We don't have to do everything. But we can follow God's calling on our hearts to do something. We will do it imperfectly, and that's OK. God is still working in the world, offering sacrificial love and grace. And when we spiral into our own concerns about relevancy, impact, or influence, God will call us out and remind us that God is still in control beyond our human understanding.

REFLECTION AND ACTION

Reflect: Consider the following questions in relation to the campaign you are planning:

Who are my actions intended to help?

What communities do I expect will be positively impacted by my actions?

Who might my actions harm?

What communities might I be ignoring or neglecting? What do my actions look like from their perspective?

Act: Once you identify who you might be harming, ignoring, or neglecting, find the resources to help you course correct. Actively seek out resources, people, or organizations that can help prevent you from making these errors.

Act: Form relationships with significantly different organizations so you can build sensitivity to other marginalized groups into your action plan.

13 | UNDERSTAND THE VALUE AND LIMITATIONS OF INSTITUTIONS

We need to spend a little time talking about institutions. I've stressed many times so far that we are much more effective at our advocacy if we work with others who align with our mission and vision and that our organizations are much more effective if we can find movement partners that can expand our scope and reach. At some point, when you have enough people interested in your cause and motivated to join or support you in some way, you will need to organize your people, your money, and your strategy.

When you get to this point, you will want to think about building an infrastructure to support your advocacy in a much more sustained and systematic way. There are larger organizations that are good at organizing people and money. Our churches and denominations have the infrastructure to make our advocacy work easier. Many of our denominations have their own advocacy offices in DC or New York. We will need to think strategically about the implications of working with any larger institution, including our own churches. Using the resources of a larger institution can enhance your work, but you need to be wise about how you use the institution.

BE WISE AS SERPENTS AND INNOCENT AS DOVES

Earlier in this book, I shared the story of our work to change the Evangelical Lutheran Church in America (ELCA) policy concerning LGBTQ clergy. Because of the debate over the ban, denomination officials were reticent to do anything that might be interpreted as endorsing our position. They wanted to look "neutral," or in churchy talk, to be "a pastoral presence." Even after the policy change was voted on and passed, denominational leaders didn't actively support the organizations and our efforts. Instead, the concern was for the people who were upset that this decision had been made.

To take it back to the continuum of acceptance I talked about in chapter 6, we had moved the institution from "punitive rejection" through "silence" and into a phase of "tolerance." It was a significant step forward for the institution, but there was a lot of fear of taking additional steps. In the case of a mainline Protestant church like the ELCA, there is a continued fear of backlash for being too vocal on LGBTQ issues. That fear may require baby steps to learn how to advocate in a way that is authentic and faithful to the institution and its values.

The primary goal of an institution is its own preservation. The calculation of risk is different when any action is evaluated through the lens of self-preservation. This can prevent actions that are deemed to be risks, even necessary risks, to the well-being of the institution. You are probably reading this and saying, "But the primary mission of the church is to spread the gospel." That is absolutely correct, but we have taken the spreading of the gospel and institutionalized it, transforming it from a ragtag bunch of disciples into a global movement complete with hierarchy, processes, and formality. The institution of the Christian church has been around for so long, we sometimes confuse it with the gospel itself. Some may be concerned that if the institution ceases, then the mechanism for being able to spread the gospel also ceases.

Institutions, like the church, have additional resources we can use in pursuit of our advocacy, and we should take advantage of those resources when they are helpful. Just as when we work with other people or organizations, our collective voice through institutions can be stronger.

Go and Do Likewise: Find out if your denomination has an advocacy office, what issues they are working on, and how they are best doing that. If their efforts can enhance your work, then figure out how to best use their resources and their access. If they are not helpful to your particular area of advocacy, then consider pushing them to speak out on your issue.

However, some of the crises we face are urgent and require quick, bold action, quicker and bolder than our institutions can move. When we know an action must be taken, we cannot wait for institutions to catch up. We need to be bold and step up into action. We will need to come up with our own resources. When we do, we will find ourselves either leading or leaving behind the institution. We have to be discerning in when and how we are going to use the institutional resources and when they are not serving our purposes.

If you are cringing at this paragraph, take a quick look at history. The Christian church has found itself both on the side of justice for the marginalized and reinforcing the oppressive systems that keep marginalized people in their place. We've seen those swings exist—from the Reformation, to Nazi Germany, to the US civil rights movement, to QAnon. All those movements were attached to the institution of the church in some form, but the expression of activity ranged widely.

CONSIDER THE IMPLICATIONS OF YOUR CONGREGATION AS AN INSTITUTION

One place to start to scale up your advocacy is within your own congregation. Even at this more basic level, you will need to formalize your process. You are no longer a group of concerned individuals meeting casually to discuss a particular issue or take a single action; you are moving into a long-term strategy. You will need to present your idea, your strategy, and your organization to the decision makers at your church, probably including the clergy and church council. There may be other influential figures within the congregation you will want to have on your side as well.

One of the benefits of being a ministry of the congregation is that you get a bigger voice. Instead of just speaking for yourself, you are now speaking for the congregation. That changes the dynamic a little. If your congregation does endorse and support your advocacy ministry, then your work grows and expands. You'll want to give the congregation and its leadership continued updates on your activities and plans. You'll want to provide communications, invitations, and directions to other congregational members who may be interested but need to be further informed.

In short, your work expands from focusing on a singular action to a singular target, to the work of integrating your action into the life of the congregation: reporting, communication, invitation, and education. You'll also now be responsible to the leadership, culture, and constraints of the congregation. At the same time, you will potentially reach more volunteers, have access to more money, and also carry the reputation of the congregation when you speak to those in power.

You will also quickly learn that much of your congregation's time, energy, and attention are not directed at your particular piece of advocacy. Congregations—and by extension church bodies—are primarily concerned with the day-to-day of ministry: weekly worship, ongoing ministries, community building, or even their own direct charity programs. It's not that they do not support your advocacy work, but it may be competing with everything else it takes to run the rest of a church. One of the realities of our world is that our congregations need to choose to deploy their limited resources among several priorities. Some priorities are financial, like paying the existing bills. Other priorities may have to do with drawing in and building community, supporting a dynamic worship experience, or improving the building. External advocacy efforts may not rate high on this list of priorities. And while you will surely have supporters within the congregation, you will have to work to get the attention and energy of leaders whose jobs pull them in other directions.

What if others don't agree with the position you've taken? We've seen congregations become split on issues of justice. You may encounter active resistance from members of the congregation or even higher-up church authorities who actively oppose your advocacy. Advocates for abortion access, LGBTQ rights, and women's rights have encountered stiff opposition from within the ranks of their own churches. The challenge then is to fight a two-fronted battle: one to convince society and political leaders to enact the changes you are seeking and another to fight off the detractors, some with considerable influence, within your own church body.

We've seen others claim that the church shouldn't take "political stances." Of course, what is deemed "political" is often in the eye of the beholder. US law bans nonprofits, including congregations, from endorsing a candidate or political party, but after that, there is a fair amount of freedom to advocate on behalf of a certain issue.

BUILD YOUR OWN INSTITUTION

You may also find that your advocacy work requires you to create your own organization. Several organizations formed in response to the 2016 election of Donald Trump, including Indivisible, which I described earlier in this book. What began as a viral manifesto turned into an organization with chapters and paid staff.

In the United States, forming a nonprofit organization makes it easier to raise money for your cause, but it also comes with layers of bureaucracy. You will have to report your activities and fundraising not to your congregation but to the IRS. If you pay staff, you have to follow employment law, add some human resources functionality, and report taxes. In short, you have now built your own institution, and a portion of your time, energy, and attention is going to go toward maintaining the institution you have created. This brings you back to what we said earlier about institutions: their primary concern is their own continuation.

An infrastructure turns your efforts into an institution. You always run the risk of re-creating the same frustrations you have with other institutions. Instead of purely focusing on your mission, you must now think about how to keep the institution running effectively and efficiently. This isn't to say that you shouldn't formalize an organization, but it's important to be aware of the risks.

On a more positive note, building an infrastructure helps you sustain the work. An infrastructure adds more people who can help carry the burden and amplify your voice. An infrastructure gives you a method for your strategy that can attract funders and volunteers. An infrastructure is necessary to keep you from taking all the burden on yourself and burning yourself out.

The other advantage of building your own advocacy organization is that you will build it with the values and goals of accomplishing a particular piece of justice instead of trying to shape it around an existing organization that may have its own priorities. You can focus your attention, energy, and effort. And if the larger institution—like the church, for example—wants to support your work, they still can. But you aren't waiting on the church to decide to make this particular action a priority.

REFLECTION AND ACTION

Reflect: Consider the implications of joining your individual advocacy to your congregation. What would be the benefits? What would you gain? What would be the challenges?

Act: Schedule a conversation with your pastor or church council leadership to discuss your advocacy, how you operate, and your thoughts about joining your efforts to the mission of the congregation. Ask for their feedback on what sort of fit that would be.

Reflect: Consider the implications of formalizing your own advocacy into an organization. What are the benefits? What are the challenges?

Act: Reach out to your fellow advocates to get their perspectives on your work and whether it needs to be formalized any further. If you can, discuss with a lawyer (pro bono, of course) what would need to be done to incorporate your work.

Reflect: As you think about your advocacy long term, how much will you dedicate to the following:
Direct action
Education
Fundraising
Volunteer management
Reporting

Act: Write up a plan that will balance your advocacy with the rest of the priorities you have in your life. Talk with your family, friends, and loved ones about this to get their perspectives.

14 | HONOR AND STRETCH YOUR LIMITS

Through our involvement with our local Indivisible chapter, my husband, Richard, and I got involved in a campaign to reform New York State's tax code. The proposed changes would relieve the burden on poor and middle-class New Yorkers and bring in revenue from the billionaires who were living and making their money in New York. This came months after the 2020 election, when we had spent considerable energy writing letters, phone banking, and working to elect progressive candidates who, we hoped, would roll back the harsh Trump-era policies that encouraged discrimination and persecution as well as pass some policies that would build economic and social stability for the vast majority of Americans who weren't millionaires or billionaires. Now that we had elected those types of leaders in New York State, it was time to advocate for a tax system and a budget that didn't fall disproportionately on the poor and working class but rather allowed for billionaires who made their money in New York to pay it forward for the blessings they had received.

Richard was especially excited to get involved, and he threw himself into activity with a passion. I followed his lead, supporting his volunteering as much as I was able. We worked with dozens of organizations across the state, checking in on Saturday-morning meetings. Richard signed us up for webinars, teach-ins, social media sharing, and occasionally bigger tasks like phone banking.

Early in the campaign, to raise awareness and support among New York voters, we signed up for an action to hang flyers on the doors of people's homes. The flyers were designed with hooks to hang them on doorknobs. The appeal was that it didn't involve door knocking and face-to-face contact (side note here to say that face-to-face conversations are the most essential, but many of us were burned out after so much phone banking and door knocking during the 2020 election cycle). We simply had to walk up to a house, hang a flyer on the door handle, and walk away—at least, that's how it was supposed to work in much of New York State. In New York City, there was an added wrinkle. Most people lived in apartment buildings, so in order to hang flyers on individual doors, we needed to get into the buildings.

One thing you should know about me is that I tend to be a rule follower and a nonconfrontational person. Not having to face strangers directly was appealing, but the idea of entering a building without being invited gave me anxiety.

We assembled on the sidewalk, got our flyers, and divided the territory we were supposed to cover. Most people who had volunteered were very excited. They talked about the challenges of trying to get into large buildings. Someone acknowledged that we might not be able to get in or that we might get kicked out. Others began suggesting solutions: claiming to be a delivery person or asking to visit another apartment in the building. One person even suggested that we attempt to follow another visitor through the doorway.

None of those ideas appealed to me. They all sounded like breaking and entering. I knew that people did it all the time, and

I knew that I was involved with a worthy cause, but it still made me nervous. Richard was much bolder and moved forward.

We approached the first building, and Richard buzzed a random apartment. Someone buzzed us in, and we climbed to the top floor and started hanging the flyers on doors. I attempted to hang the flyers without making a sound and moved as quickly as possible.

Right as I was reaching out to place the hanger on one door, it swung open. Two women were leaving and happened to catch me in the act. An alarm went off in my head that I'd been caught. Keeping it together, I smiled and said, "Hi, I'm here with a budget justice commission and urging people to call their state senators to tax the rich." I then handed them one of the flyers. They were very pleasant, said thank you, and took my flyer.

I had made it through my first crisis, but now my adrenaline was pumping. We got to the second building. This was a much larger building that required an elevator. As we exited the elevator, a resident in the hall warily eyed us. He even stalled entering the elevator to see what we were up to. As soon as he saw us start to hang flyers on the doorknobs, he started yelling. The alarm bells in my head started blaring again. I quickly exited the building, escorted by the resident the whole time.

We got to our third building and successfully got inside. I started my task, but on the first door, the hanger made the slightest sound, and a dog began to bark from inside the apartment. My alarm bells went off again. This was strike three.

We finished the building, but my heart was pounding. My anxiety was not easing with practice but rather increasing with every building we approached. I realized that this was something I just could not do. As much as I supported the campaign, I had a physical revulsion to sneaking into a building. I did not want to try to follow someone in. I did not want to get caught, and I had been three times already.

I talked with Richard and said I had hit my limit. He didn't share my anxiety but was seeing how this experience was impacting me. Eventually, we decided that we would quit. This also meant we had to face the second fear of confrontation: telling the organizer that we could not continue doing our volunteer shift. He offered some suggestions for slipping into the buildings. I had to eventually tell him I was too much of a rule follower to try to sneak into a building. He was disappointed but understood. We handed back our literature and walked away.

On the walk home, we processed what happened. I felt like I had let everyone down: the organizer, the movement, and even Richard. We could spend the rest of this chapter debating the ethics of my actions, whether the ends justified the means. But that's not the point here. Honestly, I have so much respect for people who take risks and bend the rules in pursuit of a worthy cause. I also recognize that I am not someone to bend the rules, even when I think my cause is worthy. I have to be OK with that. While I felt disappointed that I let down the cause, it also redoubled my efforts to find other ways to bring budget justice to New York State.

SAY "NO" FAITHFULLY AND HELPFULLY

By this point in the book, you might be feeling pretty overwhelmed. We live in a broken, sinful world with multilayered, complex problems that can't be solved with simple solutions or single actions. Here's the good news: we are not designed to do

everything. This is why partnerships and coalitions are so important. Others can bring resources, skills, and attitudes that we do
not have.

In any progressive movement, there will be tasks that match
our skills and our passions. But there will also be actions that
hit our limits and sometimes push past those limits. Limits are
essential because they tell us the edges of our comfort zones. It
is always important to stretch and challenge ourselves, especially
when working for a cause we believe in. I knew that I would be
uncomfortable door hanging, but I wanted to stretch myself. I
also know I don't like phone banking, but I have done it when
the stakes are high.

Saying "no," however, can also be a faithful response. It is
a way of protecting your boundaries and energy to give to the
cause. Before you just respond "no" because it's an experience
you may not enjoy, do a little discernment. Ask yourself if "no"
is coming from a place of comfort and privilege or if it is coming
from a place of scarcity or harm. Ask yourself what the stakes
are, what is gained by your participation, and what is lost if you
don't help.

Your "no" can also be accompanied by participation in a different context. When my colleagues at GLAAD participated in the
Women's March in 2017, I stayed home, in front of my computer,
compiling photos and videos from the day, writing a blog post on
our website to be shared with media outlets, and coordinating
social media responses for the organization. I wasn't marching in
the streets, but I was playing a role in the Women's March.

If there is an immediate action that you cannot take, think
about the other ways that you can contribute to the movement.
Fundraising, media engagement, logistical organization, data

entry, cooking a meal, hosting operations in your guest room, phone calls, door knocking, protesting outside of an office or driving the protesters in your vehicle, negotiating behind the scenes, and securing powerful supporters are just a few of the actions that help make a successful movement. If you are truly dedicated, you will probably do more than one thing to support the cause, combining donations and actions.

TRY "NOT NOW" INSTEAD OF "NO"

Another faithful alternative to "no" is "not now." This work is hard, and fighting for progressive ideals is constant work. It is filled with setbacks and disappointments, and it takes effort to make even the most incremental change. When we really get into a cause, we can pour our whole selves into it, using up all our energy. Just as Jesus retreated into the wilderness, we can also step away for a short period of time.

For many of us, we need to fight the urge to feel guilty about self-care. My boss at GLAAD recognized that many of us were workaholics, spending our evenings, weekends, holidays, and vacation days continuing to respond to emails, review documents, and handle whatever crisis had popped up. It made sense, since many incidents happened outside of regular office hours. However, she recognized that many of us were burning ourselves out. She didn't want to quell our energy or dedication, but she knew that we were working ourselves at an unhealthy rate. Among several reforms, she would encourage us to truly take days off. Before long holiday breaks, she would remind us of her four Rs: *rest, relax, recharge,* and more importantly, *return.* She wanted us to take a break so that we would come back and reapply ourselves to the work ahead. Her advice was designed to keep us able to focus on the long-term mission.

Go and Do Likewise: If you do need to take a break to focus on self-care, make sure that moment is truly self-care. Spend time doing something that truly nourishes you and occupies your mind. Tactile work—like cooking, handicrafts, or gardening—can use your body and mind to relieve stress. Eat healthy and comforting food. Take a walk or exercise. Think of your self-care break as a way to heal and strengthen yourself to go back into the world of advocacy.

STRETCH YOUR LIMITS

Remember, sometimes your limits will be stretched. I have discomfort with protests and rallies, but I have shown up at several such actions over the years. I don't enjoy phone banking, but I will do it for a cause that I care about or a candidate I think will advance that cause. Sometimes the need is too urgent for us to stay within our comfort zones. Sometimes we will be called to step up to fill a particular need.

We have plenty of examples in Scripture of God pushing people past their limits, handling their doubts and perceived lack of talent. Moses gave several reasons why he should not be the one to lead the Hebrew people out of Egypt, and God addressed every one of his concerns. At one point, God even divided the labor, giving his brother, Aaron, a speaking role to compliment Moses's difficulty speaking.[1]

Just like a physical workout, after you've stretched your-self, spend time healing. Congratulate yourself on pushing past your limits and doing something new. Evaluate what exactly felt like a stretch and how you handled it. Will the new action be less stressful when you do it again? In what ways can you make this easier to do? Take a breath, and then find a way to gather your strength to do the next thing that needs to be done.

You will need to balance your faithful "no" with a recognition that God may be calling you to something beyond what you imagined for yourself. It will take constant discernment and self-examination of your comfort level, energy, and skills, paired with an examination of the situation at hand, the stakes, and the risks of being involved versus the risks of not taking action.

REFLECTION AND ACTION

Reflect: Once you get into a movement, you will likely be asked to take on more responsibilities and add more to your plate. This is a sign of your growing leadership and dedication. Spend a little time in discernment. Think through the following questions to avoid burnout and to maximize the impact of your actions.

What is your capacity for further action?

Do you have the time to participate in further action?

Do you have the energy to take on additional action?

Do you have the spiritual and emotional capacity to take on additional action?

What is the impact of your participation?

What will your contribution to this specific action add to the movement?

Are you uniquely situated to offer tangible help and assistance?

What will be the cost of your lack of participation?

What are the stakes?

Is the situation urgent enough that personal discomfort must be set aside?

Who is going to be helped by this action?

Who is going to be hurt by not taking action?

How else might you be able to contribute?

Are there alternative actions you can take that will still be helpful?

Are there other people you can invite to join you in the action?

What is God calling you to do in this particular moment?

Act: Clearly communicate to others both your interest and your boundaries in working on this particular area of advocacy. Letting others know your capacity helps them plan their actions more accurately. Perhaps they can recruit others, or perhaps they can tweak their expectations to match what you are able to give. The important thing is to stay in constant communication about your own capacity.

15 | PUT A FACE TO THE ISSUE, BUT NOT ALWAYS YOURS

We cannot deny that we live in a world where information, messaging, and media are ubiquitous. One of the most effective ways to reach people and impact them viscerally so that they do something is to put a "face" to an issue—that is, demonstrate the real, concrete harm that is happening to real, everyday people. Generally, as humans, we don't conceptualize ideas very well. But once we understand an issue through the lens of personal experience, we can relate and possibly act to solve the problem. This is where storytelling becomes important. We can use stories and personal anecdotes that explain how we or others are being harmed by the current situation. Personal stories hit people emotionally rather than rationally. They feel compassion, or literally "suffering with" us, as we relay how we've been harmed.

When I was working at ReconcilingWorks, we trained our participants to use stories as a way to move hearts and minds. When I moved on to GLAAD, we taught people the same storytelling techniques to reach their target audience through the media. Both of these trainings were based on the public narrative work of Marshall Ganz at Harvard University. Ganz developed a process to reach people through different types of stories: story of self, story of us, and story of now.[1]

You can check out Ganz or sign up for trainings through GLAAD, ReconcilingWorks, or many other advocacy organizations. However, what I want to focus on here is the use of stories to move people into action. As part of my training at GLAAD, I let people know that personal stories are the most compelling, as they are relatable and come with a personal passion.

When people hear personal stories, they are moved in their gut, which is then processed through the heart and eventually rationalized through the mind. When people react emotionally to our stories, they are most primed to digest and believe what we are telling and also the most likely to do something about it. That is when you want to give them a tangible action step. They now feel, in their gut, what the problem is, and they will be motivated to do something to solve it.

USE SOCIAL MEDIA (CAREFULLY!) AS A TOOL FOR ADVOCACY

Social media has made it easier to put faces and stories to issues. Through social media, we can reach a wider swath of people to demonstrate how something is harming us personally or someone we care about. We talked about social media earlier in this book, but it's worth revisiting in this context.

Social media allows people to become their own media outlet, reporting on the world around them and creating visibility without waiting for gatekeepers to allow their presence. We can raise visibility for the people and the issues that are ignored by mainstream media. And for many, being visible and vocal is an act of advocacy and resistance in a world that tries to erase our existence.

There is no doubt that social media has changed the advocacy game. We can reach more people and connect with others who are working on the same issues. The filming and broadcasting of police brutality has made others aware of and, at a minimum, forced Americans to face an unpleasant truth about racism in our country. As I'm writing this, images of the Russian invasion of Ukraine are flooding my social media feed, as well as photos, videos, and stories of heroic Ukrainian resistance. Without social media, the information and images we receive would be filtered through some other source, one that decides what we "should" see and know. There is a great democratizing aspect to getting to witness things from a personal perspective.

On the flip side, however, social media has also exploited our natural narcissism, blurring the lines between what we share for the good of our cause and what we share in order to show ourselves, whether it is promoting our actions, broadcasting our opinions and hot takes, or securing our positions as experts and leaders. You may have heard terms like *slacktivism* or *performative* when applied to symbolic actions or social media engagement that doesn't actually do anything beyond achieving visibility for the poster.

Performative slacktivism reminds me of a parable Jesus told about a father who sent his two sons to work in his vineyard. The first said, "I will not," but he eventually went to do the work. The second son said, "I go, sir," but he never actually went to work in the fields. Jesus asked which son did the will of the father, and the crowd answered, "The first."[2] This story can apply to so many aspects of our advocacy but can also be true of social media posting that looks good but doesn't change anything.

Compounding social media's tendency to feed into narcissism, our Western culture has a lot of big personalities. There are figures who capture our attention by saying the most provocative things. Attention has been treated as currency, and people find ways to capture it through any means possible. We've heard the outlandish statements of social media influencers, podcast hosts, media personalities, and even elected officials. They make provocative statements to ensure we are paying attention to them, talking about them, and thinking about them. These outlandish figures can come from the right or the left or often are a strange mix of the two. Their goal is to keep an audience. That same attention-seeking toxic mentality can easily creep into our own advocacy, distracting us from the issue at hand and turning our attention to counting social media followers, impressions, and engagements.

I try to remind advocates that social media is a tool. I can use a hammer to repair a step, and I can also hit you on the head with it. The tool's proper use helps accomplish good things, while misuse causes tremendous harm. We have to treat social media like a dangerous tool that needs to be handled with proper care. From the perspective of the social media platform, the main goal is to keep you using it as much as possible. That goal does not necessarily line up with your goal of God's justice in a particular form.

BEWARE OF PRACTICING YOUR PIETY BEFORE OTHERS

Jesus had something else to say about big media personalities who focus more on their brand than on impact. In Matthew 6, he warns the people around him, "Beware of practicing your piety before others in order to be seen by them; for then you have no reward from your Father in heaven." Jesus was addressing those who were flouting their religiosity for the admiration of others, but he also made it apply to those who were providing charity:

"Whenever you give alms, do not sound a trumpet before you, as the hypocrites do in the synagogues and in the streets, so that they may be praised by others. Truly I tell you, they have received their reward."[3] If we are working for accolades from others, then we are not truly advocating for the poor and marginalized.

We live in a world where our lives and our actions are easily recordable and sharable. To be perfectly honest, sharing teachable moments may have value. Maybe our words and actions can reach someone to inspire and educate them. But we can easily fall into the trap of making the issue about us, promoting our actions and telling people (and God) how "good" we are. It's where the word *performative* comes in.

The danger, of course, is that we turn ourselves into the institution we discussed in the previous chapter, where the main goal is the advancement and preservation of ourselves and our "brand." If we are doing advocacy to make ourselves look good, then we are doing it wrong.

There is also another practical danger in this. When we set ourselves up for kudos from others, there is less incentive for them to participate. It reinforces the belief that we have it handled, and they won't need to do anything. Even at those moments when we might get attention for our work, we want to invite others to join us and participate where and how they can.

A church group asked my husband and me to give a talk about the various forms of advocacy we participate in. It seemed like good preparation for this book, so we said yes. During the short talk, we rattled off many of the organizations we were a part of, telling stories of the actions and campaigns we had supported. Finally, one woman spoke up and said, "But you do such amazing things! I could never do all that." Our stories, meant to

inspire her into finding a way to take action, had actually intimidated her back into believing she was helpless, the opposite of
what we intended.

Jesus caps off this teaching with this: "When you give alms,
do not let your left hand know what your right hand is doing, so
that your alms may be done in secret; and your Father who sees
in secret will reward you." So what is the twenty-first-century
equivalent of not letting your right hand know what your left
hand is doing? A great question to ask ourselves would be, "What
if I did an amazing thing that advanced my cause and no one
knew I was behind it?" We may get no credit for our actions, no
matter how noble, and we have to be OK with that.

USE YOUR PLATFORM TO LIFT UP OTHERS

There are two types of people we should constantly be lifting up
and promoting through our advocacy efforts, especially those of
us who live relatively privileged lives. The first group is the people
who are doing incredible work, especially when their work is over-
looked. The second is the people whose lives and livelihoods are
most impacted by the issues at hand.

When you look, you will find significant overlap between
these two groups. The best stories to share are from people who
belong to both of these groups. Inequality exacerbates the issues
we face, with a disproportionate impact falling upon marginalized groups like people of color, immigrants, people with disabilities, LGBTQ people, and people in poverty. Marginalized
communities do incredibly well at surviving, thriving, and organizing to make change but often are not recognized or offered
the benefit of support from mainstream institutions. They also

often know best the future they wish to see and how to build that future. We can listen to them and amplify their calls for justice in whatever form that may take.

One word of warning about lifting up marginalized groups is that they must be given the power to tell their own stories, not those we want to tell for them. Self-determination and consent are important when lifting up the stories of others. When we exploit someone else's story, we again make it all about us. Instead of exploiting a story that you can amplify and make your own, look for one that is already out there.

By highlighting their work, we are giving our endorsement for others to see them as experts and leaders in the movement. Instead of allowing ourselves to be portrayed as saviors, we can point to Christ as the savior for all of humanity. We can recognize the Holy Spirit, who is already working among marginalized communities, making a better world for all of God's creation. We can also give thanks to God for others who are doing the work to advance justice in their own particular ways.

> **Go and Do Likewise:** Sign up for the email newsletter of an organization run by a marginalized community so you can get direct communication from them on their priorities and how you can support their work. When you get the newsletter, use your social media to quote what the organization is saying about a particular issue. Encourage your social media followers to also support the organization and its leaders. Be sure to constantly lift up the organization and its leaders by name, providing a link for others to visit their site.

Constant self-examination of ourselves and our motivations is important so that we know why we do what we do. There is nothing wrong with recognition, and in some cases, it helps advance visibility for our cause. But when it becomes our sole motivator, then it takes away from the goals we are trying to accomplish.

Paradoxically, there may also be times when we are encouraged to be more visible and vocal so that we can encourage others, and we have to be OK with that too. Sometimes, we are the ones who can reach a certain audience. We can use that privilege to give access to others. That might mean taking a meeting with an elected official alongside someone who is more directly impacted or a group that doesn't have the level of access we have. It may mean sharing information with others so they can be motivated to take action for themselves. Sometimes, that will mean giving an explicit call to action, telling people, step by step, what we did and how they can take the same actions.

What is important is that our visibility is not about us but about the cause we are working for. If asked why we took an action, combine sharing personal reasons why we care with a call for others who care just as much to also act. We talk about the injustice that is happening and how collectively we can fix it. Even when we make ourselves visible, we don't have to make the issue all about ourselves. The best version of this storytelling has been along the lines of, "I was unaware of this issue. After someone opened my eyes to it, I felt I needed to do something to help. I invite you to join us in solving this issue."

We are putting ourselves and our reputations out there as we do this advocacy, but this is not about us. This is about the grace that God pours upon us, allowing everyone to live full, abundant lives. This is about the people who are still being blocked from full, abundant lives because of a myriad of sins, including bigotry, exploitation, inequality, greed, and lust for power. Our advocacy is about us using the grace and the privilege that have been afforded us to make the world better for others.

REFLECTION AND ACTION

Reflect: Every time you seek visibility for your work, spend a little time in self-examination. Think about what you are doing, why you are doing it, and what the rewards will be for the cause you are advancing. The following questions can help you discern whether you are advancing your cause or engaging in self-promotion:

What is my goal in sharing this? Will it reach people who can also act?

How much of what I'm sharing is about the issue at hand versus about me and my actions?

Who is most directly impacted by the issue I'm working on? Can I lift up their story?

Who else is working on this that I can use my platform to promote?

Act: Cite your sources. When you share information about an issue, uplift a personal story, or amplify a campaign, be sure to thank and endorse the person or organization that provided the information. If you are supporting the actions of a marginalized group, provide an opportunity along with some encouragement for others to also support that group. Demonstrate this by paying marginalized groups for their time and teaching.

16 | LIVE YOUR ADVOCACY ON A DAILY BASIS

Remember how at the beginning of this book, I said that I never intended to be an activist? To be honest, I still feel like I'm figuring it all out. Our world is broken and sinful in so many ways, and there are so many people and organizations trying to solve our problems. I continue to be in awe of those activists who are making real-world impacts through their actions. My focus has been on the intersection between LGBTQ advocacy and faith, but that is only one area of focus. The interconnections of the LGBTQ community overlap with every other aspect of our human life on earth. That means I need to care about everything else. At a minimum, I need to avoid inadvertently harming partner movements by my actions.

As I grow and become more aware of the complexity of the issues surrounding us, I'm learning that I cannot think of advocacy as something that I add to the demands of my daily routine; rather, I must think of it as something I live out through every aspect of my daily life. It becomes naturally integrated into every decision I make, every action I take, every relationship I form. Our values are reflected in every choice we make. They show up in our purchases, our messages, and our interactions.

In short, it becomes a lifestyle.

We live in a world of systemic sin. We participate in racism, sexism, exploitation, xenophobia, homophobia, transphobia, ableism, and so many other sins without even realizing what we are doing. It will take constant self-examination to learn how we can disrupt those systems in our own lives and in the communities and cultures in which we participate. We also know that we are human, born in sin, and cannot fully justify ourselves. Our actions and advocacy are not about justifying ourselves; rather, they're about using the grace God has given us to allow everyone to live freely.

After the 2016 election, so many of us were in despair, without a really clear direction of what to do. It seemed like everything that we had been working for was about to be dashed. The progress we had built seemed in peril. Environmentalists worried about the government changing regulations to make it easier to exploit the earth. Women worried about their freedoms and futures. Immigrants, people of color, LGBTQ people, and other marginalized groups instantly felt a target on their backs. I needed to put what had changed with that election into perspective and focus on what I could control. I started writing a document that looked at both immediate and long-term needs. One thing that struck me as I put the document together was that the actions I was proposing weren't very different from what I would have recommended before the election. It was just that the context had shifted and made those actions more urgent. This final chapter takes those suggestions as a template for how we might live out our values in the everyday choices we make.

FOCUS ON WHERE YOUR MONEY GOES

The first place to examine is where and how you spend your money. In a capitalist economy like we have in the United States, money signifies priorities. The money we give to a business indicates how much of a necessity the item is or how much we value it.

Better World Shopper is a book and a website[1] that has developed a great ranking system for companies in all sorts of industries. It grades them on five factors: human rights, the environment, animal protection, community involvement, and social justice.

There are other lists that track corporate behavior on a variety of issues. The organization Accountable for Equality Action created the Real Allies Database to track corporate contributions to legislators who work to curtail the rights and protections of the US population. The organization monitors four categories: pro-insurrection, anti-LGBTQ, anti-choice, and anti–voting rights.[2] Even more specifically, the Human Rights Campaign has the Corporate Responsibility Index, measuring LGBTQ inclusion, protections, and advocacy in companies.[3] Often lists like these are built in response to specific situations. The Moral Rating Agency was created after Russia's 2022 invasion of Ukraine.[4] It records public corporations' responses to the invasion, letting consumers and advocates know who has pulled out and who is staying in. Grab Your Wallet was formed after the 2016 release of the *Access Hollywood* tape that included vulgar and sexist comments by Donald Trump.[5] It demonstrated women's spending power and ensured that money wasn't inadvertently spent to support the Trump Organization or administration. Since then, the campaign has broadened to target unethical corporate practices and promote equity throughout the company.

Beyond those lists, there are a few additional things that can help. As much as possible, buy local and avoid large national chains. One way to measure this for yourself is to ask if you can identify and build a relationship with the owner. You may pay more locally because small businesses often can't secure the bulk deals that large corporations can, but your money stays within the community and is much more likely to come back to the benefit of your local community and its needs. When you shop at a national chain, your money is moved out of the community to wherever the headquarters are and often paid to the executives and shareholders.

According to Better World Shopper, one of the most impactful choices you can make is where you do your banking and financial transactions.[6] Banks work with your money, whether or not you are actively spending. Large banks and financial firms tend to finance a lot of corporations that violate your values. Local banks keep your money local, and credit unions are designed to benefit a specific population, giving the interest earned on your money back into the membership. That means banking with a local bank or credit union will multiply your impact when you are spending or when you are saving.

There are some local businesses that will have politics or values that do not align with yours. You may not want your spending money to go toward funding activities that are working directly against your advocacy. This may present a conundrum: either you patronize a business whose values you don't support or you spend your money outside the local economy.

It is possible that your relationship with the business can make you influence their worldview, moving them from a position of punitive rejection or silence into tolerance or acceptance. It's hard to remember, but those can be considered steps forward. If you completely withdraw your presence and your witness, then they may be left in an echo chamber of messages that will continue them down the path of punitive rejection.

Only you know where that line is. If anyone's safety, including your own, is at risk, then you are under no obligation to continue to patronize the business. You also have to be ready to be a witness, sharing your values and the stories that shape your advocacy when you meet. This doesn't mean a confrontation or debate every time, but it does mean avoiding messaging or framing traps and also actively offering your own messages. Think of the stories that are happening in the news or in your own life that help reinforce your worldview, and have them ready if the conversation goes there.

As much as you can, spend your money at businesses owned by women, people of color, people with disabilities, or LGBTQ people. In many cases, people of color build their businesses on personal funds and labor, as many minority-owned businesses haven't been afforded financial protections at the same rate as white-owned businesses.[7]

Watch out for the traps of price and convenience, which often make it harder to shop and do your business locally. National chains have the ability to undercut local businesses on prices, absorbing the loss in the short term. In our early attempts to shop locally, we found that Amazon had lower prices on many items. That, paired with the convenience of having an item show up at our door, made Amazon a tempting option. But sometimes price and convenience can be a temporary illusion. My husband, Richard, is an analytic shopper, comparing prices. He has noticed that disruptive tech companies, including Amazon and Uber, have stopped being the less expensive options in many instances. He also found that the convenience that tech companies promised now only exists at a premium level that requires an extra fee.

One other thing to consider, which can have a substantial impact: subscribe to a farm share through a program called community-supported agriculture (CSA), which allows you to buy seasonal food directly from a local farm.[8] The benefits are plentiful. Farmers get funding earlier to help them market, manage cash flow more easily, and also cover any unforeseen weather that may damage their planned crops. When we purchase food through a CSA, we eat healthy, seasonal food, often grown with organic practices. The food is more local than grocery store products, which are often imported from other regions of the world.

While each farm-share subscription is a little different, this is how many of them work: You pay for a "season" of vegetables in advance. You receive a weekly box of vegetables from the farm. The money goes to a local farmer, keeping the money in the local economy. The food is transported a much shorter distance, saving emissions from travel. Even the act of participation will alter your lifestyle a little. Picking up fresh produce means you will be preparing your meals at home, making healthier meals with fewer preservatives and chemical flavorings. Sometimes, you'll get a new food you are unfamiliar with, expanding your culinary horizons. And there is a social element. Often, at the farm-share pick-up site, members mingle, sharing recipes and building community around the food they are all supporting. You will also find that the food tastes amazing. As Americans, we have gotten very used to bland food, heightened with sugar and salt. But the natural flavors of vegetables will astound you. I often end up eating many of the vegetables raw just so I can experience their natural flavors.

> **Go and Do Likewise:** Build a moral budget. Look at how your money is spent. Take note of who is actually getting paid and what they do with your money. As mentioned, where we do our more essential financial transactions can make a huge difference, so evaluate your banking and utility bills. Also look at what charitable and political contributions you are making. See if there are ways to make adjustments to where you spend your money and how you contribute.

CONSUME GOOD INFORMATION

We also need to talk about consuming good information and fighting disinformation. I spent a lot of time talking about our worldviews. Worldviews are not easily changed, but constant reinforcement can shift or harden them. Since the 2016 election, we have had a lot of conversations about "fake news" and the role that social media has in spreading misinformation. We've been exposed to constant misinformation about the coronavirus, the 2020 election, the curriculum being taught in schools, crime and policing, the economic impact of the wealthy versus the working class, and so much more just within the past couple of years. Of course, propaganda isn't new, but social media adds a whole new dimension. It allows anyone to become a propagandist, sometimes even inadvertently.

Be on guard against consuming propaganda, especially if that news confirms your existing worldview and elicits an emotional reaction. Social media is convenient. It allows any information (true or not) to be consumed and shared incredibly quickly, leaving little time for critical thinking or further research. At its core, propaganda is designed to spark outrage, clicks, and shares.

This means you need to put reasonable limits on social media consumption, which has been how so much disinformation and propaganda spreads. Do it for your mental health as well as to ensure access to quality information.

If you see someone sharing misinformation or disinformation, please gently tell the poster when they share fake or misleading sources, even if you agree with the sentiment. You can also direct them to better sources of information. This is a courtesy for them as well as for you. It also helps develop a list of media that you do trust to be fair and accurate. Find not just media sources that confirm your existing biases, political or otherwise, but ones that do investigative journalism and analysis (not just talking points from political parties). There is a difference between news with a political leaning (conservative or liberal) and disinformation, and this distinction is essential. And even the most trusted news outlets often get information or framing wrong, especially in a fast-moving media moment.

It is helpful to order a paid subscription to your local news outlet. Local news has been shrinking over the past several years, but it is the foundation of the ecosystem of information. You want to know what is happening in your city or state. You want to hear what is being discussed at school board meetings and city council meetings. You want to hear about the tragedies and joys your neighbors are experiencing. It makes you a good neighbor, in a real, tangible relationship with the people who live closest to you. It also helps to understand the local reactions to national or international news. Sometimes, the impact of an event or trend is different for your local economy and culture than it will be elsewhere, and it's good to be connected to that.

In addition, you should participate in local media as much as possible. Use your local media to let your neighbors know what you believe and why. Submit op-eds and letters to the editor of your local newspaper. Call reporters with tips and suggestions for story ideas. If you are an expert in something, let them know you are an available resource. You can influence your local media as well as your local community on the issues that are important to you and reach more people to join your movement. The impact of your messages coming across in the local media is much greater than a simple social media post, but you can turn your media hit into a social media post to extend its reach.

Add to your reading list publications that focus on communities outside your own. Follow some trusted outlets that focus on the LGBTQ, Black, Latinx, disability, or other communities that often don't get covered by the mainstream press.[9] You will find stories that you didn't know existed and probably be better informed about what is happening to and within those communities.

STRENGTHEN DEMOCRACY THROUGH CIVIC ENGAGEMENT

Finally, we need to participate in democracy, constantly. In the United States, it feels like we are in a never-ending election cycle. The media often focuses on the horse race side of the news, talking about it as a fight between two political parties. You can transcend this perspective by remembering your worldview and the goals of your advocacy. We elect people not so that a political party can have power but so that we can advance our values in real, tangible ways. We want political leaders who will enact helpful laws and policies or, at a minimum, defend against laws and policies that will move our cause backward. That is not about political parties but about values.

Participation in democracy means voting in every single election. Primary elections are where we can most easily vote in alignment with our values, since we have a wider range of choices. The general election often has fewer options and may involve voting with the candidate on the ballot who is the most likely to advance our values. Runoff and special elections have just as much impact and are often determined by a handful of votes. But the results have a tremendous impact on our lives. The more local the election, the more direct the impact.

You can and should strategically get involved with political campaigns for candidates who align with your values and seem the most likely to act upon them. They will be the ones who may help advance your advocacy and drive real-world impact.

You can also support democracy by supporting nonpartisan voter registration drives and encouragement for every eligible citizen to vote. Another powerful, temporary job you can take is that of an election worker. Election workers keep democracy running by making the voting process go quicker and easier. As we've seen in recent elections, we need election workers with integrity. It could be you. Consider taking on a temporary job helping democracy continue in the United States.

In between elections, we should continue to be in touch with our elected leaders. If they agree with you, thank them and encourage them to be bold leaders who bring their peers along.

If they are on the fence, let them know why you think they should take action that supports your position. If they are in opposition, let them know they are out of step with their constituency. Remind them that another election is always coming, and you are looking for an elected leader who will act to make this a better, more just and equitable world.

LIVE A LIFESTYLE OF GOSPEL JUSTICE

I have to end by being clear. None of these things by themselves will solve the brokenness of the world. As I said, the problems we face are legion, and the responses to help people cope with inequity as well as make things better will take a multiplicity of perspectives, utilizing a variety of actions. And, of course, new problems will arise.

There really is no short-term fix. That's where our advantage as Christians comes in. We are taught stories about God's relationship with a broken and sinful humanity that spans millennia. We see the advancements and setbacks documented in the Bible, which often mirror our own world. While the particular issues confronted in the Bible may not totally match what we are facing today, we can see same types of emotions and responses spelled out. That gives us a vision for our own attitudes and how we can try to match God's long-term vision for the world God created.

All the things I've mentioned in this chapter are lifestyle changes. They are to be incorporated into our daily routine, changing the way we interact with the world around us. Even our small actions can have ripple effects. We sometimes assume that changing the world for the better involves extraordinary action. But there is no magic solution to the troubles the world is facing. It will require a constant, prayerful examination of our actions, our choices, and our budgets.

And occasionally, just occasionally, God will call us to an extraordinary task. It will be something we never imagined for ourselves, but the Holy Spirit will give us the strength and guidance to continue, imperfectly. And the grace of God will carry us through. And when we are done running this race, we will be greeted with "Well done, good and faithful servant."

That is my prayer.

REFLECTION AND ACTION

Reflect: This whole chapter is a long list of suggestions. Make a list of every suggestion in the chapter, and include a few that you think of that I didn't mention.

Act: Start out slowly. Choose one thing that you can incorporate into your daily life and routine, and start to implement it. Once you feel like you have that one thing down, add something else.

Reflect: Don't settle for one action, but don't get overwhelmed by a lot of lifestyle changes all at once. What is the next best lifestyle change to incorporate into your daily routine? "Best" in this instance is a combination of what is achievable and what has the most impact.

Act: Repeat these reflections and actions until you've started doing transformational work with high-impact actions, both within your own personal lifestyle and also in collaboration with other people and organizations that are working to make this world a better place.

APPENDIX

Resources to Help Your Advocacy

Don't feel like you have to start from nothing. Many denominations have advocacy offices in Washington, DC, or near the United Nations. It is worth connecting with your own denomination's advocacy program and seeing if its objectives match up with yours. If not, don't worry. Let these organizations and resources help connect you with where you are feeling called.

I want to start by highlighting a few of the organizations and resources referenced in this book. They are the work of friends and colleagues, people who saw a need and figured out a way to fill it.

Better World Shopper

betterworldshopper.org

This resource, both a website and a book, is a public research project dedicated to making social and environmental data available to consumers who want to make wise choices about where and how they spend their money in order to help build a better world.

Center for Artistic Activism

c4aa.org

This organization combines art and activism, using the best of each to think strategically about how to use the beauty of creativity and the tenacity of activism to call attention to an issue or usher in progressive social change.

GLAAD

glaad.org

I've been a GLAAD staff member for over a decade, helping to shape fair, accurate, and inclusive media representation for the LGBTQ community, leading to awareness, understanding, and acceptance of LGBTQ people.

Indivisible

indivisible.org

Indivisible's manifesto inspired millions to form local political and civic engagement organizations around the country and gave tangible action steps when things seemed bleak after the 2016 election. Its chapters all over the country encourage members to take strategic actions to resist the anti-democracy agenda, elect local champions, and fight for progressive policies.

LocalHarvest

localharvest.org

LocalHarvest is the organization I have used to find farm shares and local community-supported agriculture. It connects people looking for good, local, organic food with the farmers who produce it.

Mobilizing Our Brothers Initiative (MOBI)

mobi-nyc.com

DaShawn Usher joined other Black queer leaders to form MOBI. The organization creates a series of curated social connectivity events for gay and queer people of color to see their holistic selves while promoting community, wellness, and personal development.

Points of Light Music

pointsoflightmusic.net

Conie Borchardt is an entrepreneur who has used her skills in music and movement to build community. Her advocacy spirit led her to create several worthy programs that build community, raise marginalized voices, and enact liberation. I'll highlight two particular programs here:

- I talked about Biracial and Rural in this book. It is a community of care and a storytelling space where Black, Indigenous, and people of color who live or have lived in rural spaces are nurtured and empowered to build sustaining communal resources for healing, well-being, and support.

- Freeing Refrains is a storytelling and conversation space where participants examine questions like, "What binds us?" and "What liberates us?" The community is designed to be both nurturing and provocative, invoking gentle curious probing and fierce beautiful truth.

Poor People's Campaign: A National Call for Moral Revival

poorpeoplescampaign.org

This organization is a continuation of the movement started by Rev. Dr. Martin Luther King Jr. Its goals are confronting systemic racism, poverty, ecological devastation, militarism, and the war economy. The organization emphatically opposes any distorted narrative that uses religion to uphold nationalism.

Public Religion Research Institute (PRRI)
prri.org

If you need data to help support your advocacy, PRRI provides incredible independent research at the intersection of religion, culture, and public policy. Use its rigorous and trusted polling data to inform what everyday Americans know (and think they know) about the pressing issues of our day.

Repairers of the Breach
breachrepairers.org

Founded by Rev. William Barber, this organization builds a moral agenda that uses religious language to remind our elected leaders and every American of our constitutional values and how those impact our society's treatment of the poor, women, LGBTQ people, children, workers, immigrants, communities of color, and the sick—the people whom Jesus calls "the least of these."

FAITHFUL ADVOCACY ORGANIZATIONS

There are faith-based organizations of every stripe doing both advocacy and direct service work. These organizations have particular religious motivations for doing what they do and will often employ theology in their mission.

American Atheists

atheists.org

Yes, atheists do advocacy too! This organization focuses on the separation of church and state established in the First Amendment to the Constitution. Its advocacy protects religious freedom for all Americans, no matter their faith or absence of faith.

Americans United for Separation of Church and State

au.org

Americans United is another organization that ensures religious freedom by advocating for the separation between religion and the functioning of government.

Auburn Seminary

auburnseminary.org

Not a traditional seminary, Auburn equips faith leaders with organizational skills, strategic resources, and spiritual resilience so that they can have an impact on their local communities, on the national stage, and around the world.

Bend the Arc

bendthearc.us

Bend the Arc is a Jewish organization focused on advancing progressive social change in the United States. It fights white nationalism and anti-Semitism while protecting individual civil rights and democracy as a whole.

Be the Bridge

bethebridge.com

Latasha Morrison is a Christian coach and facilitator who founded Be the Bridge in 2016 to promote racial unity in the United States. The organization's main strategies include inspiring people to respond to racial division, equipping them with skills for racial healing, and partnering with other organizations focused on racial justice.

Catholics for Choice

catholicsforchoice.org

This organization represents the majority of Catholics who believe in reproductive freedom, despite what messages come from the Roman Catholic hierarchy. The organization understands the intersectionality of women's health care, also focusing on gender equality, health care access, and religious freedom.

Center for Popular Democracy

populardemocracy.org

The Center's agenda is pro-worker and pro-immigrant, advocating for racial and economic justice. Its strategy is similar to the tenets of this book: building alliances with organizations working in the same space, waging impactful campaigns, and equipping everyday people to take action.

Charter for Compassion

charterforcompassion.org

This is a charter—that is, a statement of principles for morality that uplifts and affirms our common humanity and against the use of religion for selfish gain. Anyone can sign on to the charter, and the organization offers follow-up actions to help live out the principles therein.

Christians for Social Action
christiansforsocialaction.org

Christians for Social Action describes its members as "scholar-activists." It combines biblical scholarship with policy analysis to further racial, economic, and ecological justice.

Emgage
emgageusa.org

Emgage politically organizes Muslims in America as a voting bloc, building civic participation and understanding of voting power.

Faith Forward
faith-forward.net

Children's and youth ministry has changed since the 1950s. Faith Forward helps reimagine what effective ministry looks like, addressing the challenges we face today while drawing on the foundations of theology and Scripture.

Faithful America
faithfulamerica.org

The primary tools of Faithful America are rapid-response digital campaigns and petitions calling for specific changes either in policy, practice, or culture from a progressive religious standpoint or in response to breaking news.

Faithful Democracy
faithfuldemocracy.us

This organization is a multifaith community of congregations, faith-based organizations, and religious leaders with a mission to both preserve and fix US democracy. Its work is centered on meaningful reform, including care of creation, civil rights, and voter protections.

Faith in Action
faithinaction.org

Faith in Action is an example of faith-based community-organizing networks, connecting progressive causes around the United States and equipping people of faith to fight for justice and work toward a more equitable society.

Faith in Public Life
faithinpubliclife.org

The media plays a significant role in how we understand the relationship among faith, politics, policy, and culture. Faith in Public Life is a media organization ensuring that the diversity of faith, especially the progressive side of faith, is fairly represented.

Faiths United to Prevent Gun Violence
faiths-united.org

Religious leaders formed a coalition of more than fifty faith-based organizations representing tens of millions of religious Americans seeking laws and policies to prevent gun violence. The organization calls for criminal background checks on gun sales, a civilian ban on high-capacity weapons and ammunition magazines, and the criminalization of gun trafficking.

Friends Committee on National Legislation

fcnl.org

Formed by the Quakers, the Friends Committee on National Legislation pairs denominational lobbyists on Capitol Hill with a grassroots network to advance peace, justice, and environmental stewardship.

Interfaith Alliance

interfaithalliance.org

Interfaith Alliance is a multifaith organization that champions both religion and democracy. Its work focuses on education and interfaith dialogue, election monitoring, grassroots activism to mobilize individuals, and national policy making that protects both religious freedom and democracy.

Interfaith Power & Light

interfaithpowerandlight.org

Focusing on environmental protection and climate change, Interfaith Power & Light has built out a network of affiliate organizations across the country, representing twenty-two thousand faith communities motivated to protect God's creation.

Justice Revival

justicerevival.org

Justice Revival was formed in response to religion being used to oppress rather than support human rights. Its work focuses on education about human rights from a faith-based perspective, collaboration between faith-based and secular human rights groups, and advocacy from a justice-focused human rights perspective.

Law, Rights, and Religion Project at Columbia Law School

lawrightsreligion.law.columbia.edu

As you can see, this is a think tank connected to the law school at Columbia University. It analyzes how religious liberty interacts with other human rights through the lens of social justice, freedom of religion, and religious pluralism.

Muslim Advocates

muslimadvocates.org

Muslim Advocates works for the freedom and protection of Muslim Americans. It provides "know your rights" resources to everyday Muslims as well as mobilizes against hate crimes, law enforcement bias, and famously, Trump's Muslim travel ban.

National Council of Jewish Women

ncjw.org

Driven by Jewish values, this organization focuses on the safety and well-being of women, children, and families. Its work has evolved over the years, now focusing on reproductive health, voting protection and promotion, and fair, independent, and qualified judges on federal courts.

NETWORK Lobby for Catholic Social Justice

networklobby.org

Remember the Nuns on the Bus? This is them! NET-WORK was founded by Catholic sisters in the spirit of the progressive reforms of the Second Vatican Council. The group focuses on economic justice, advocating that those at the margins are supported and those blessed with abundance should pay their fair share to ensure a prosperous society.

Network of Spiritual Progressives

spiritualprogressives.org

This network of spiritual progressives seeks to transform our materialistic and corporate-dominated culture into a loving and just society. It is the interfaith publisher of *Tikkun*, known for integrating spiritual practice and economic social justice.

Red Letter Christians

redletterchristians.org

In 2007, Tony Campolo and Shane Claiborne founded Red Letter Christians out of alarm that Western Christianity had lost its focus on Jesus and that *evangelical* only referred to a voting bloc. They began writing, speaking, and campaigning on the "good news" that evangelism is supposed to bring to the poor and oppressed.

Religious Action Center of Reform Judaism

rac.org

This organization mobilizes Reform Jews at the federal, state, and local levels to advocate for legislation on more than seventy socioeconomic issues, including gun violence prevention, immigration, reproductive rights, and criminal justice reform.

Religious Coalition for Reproductive Choice

rcrc.org

The Religious Coalition for Reproductive Choice advocates for religious liberty using the culture and values of religion with a specific focus on reproductive health care, abortion, and contraception access.

Sadhana: Coalition of Progressive Hindus

sadhana.org

Sadhana is an American Hindu organization that engages in the practice of *sadhana*, or faith in action, by advocating for the social justice principles embedded in Hinduism. That faith in action looks like service, community transformation, and advocacy work.

Sikh Coalition

sikhcoalition.org

The Sikh Coalition was formed as a volunteer organization in the trauma of a Sikh man being blamed and murdered for the September 11 attacks on the World Trade Center. Today, it works in communities, classrooms, and Congress to protect religious freedom and eliminate religious bigotry.

Sojourners

sojo.net

Sojourners is a print and online magazine for progressive Christians. It expands out into social campaigns that focus on racial justice, climate justice, economic justice, democracy, human rights, poverty, immigration, nonviolence, and women's empowerment.

White House Office of Faith Based and Community Partnerships

This office was established by George W. Bush and has continued through the following administrations, although the nature and focus of it have changed from administration to administration. It works with leaders of different faiths and backgrounds, providing updates on the White House actions and priorities and resources to empower local action.

Wild Goose Festival

wildgoosefestival.org

If you like camping, music, arts, and social justice, and just a touch of mayhem, this might be the place for you. The Wild Goose Festival is a four-day outdoor festival focused on spirituality, worship, justice, music, and arts. It features loads of high- and low-profile speakers, authors, and performers addressing their areas of specialty.

ADVOCACY ORGANIZATIONS THAT INCLUDE FAITH PROGRAMS

Center for American Progress

americanprogress.org/team/faith

The Center for American Progress is a policy institute advancing progressive ideas. The religion and faith program puts a religious perspective on the political and contemporary issues the United States is facing.

Human Rights Campaign

hrc.org/resources/religion-faith

The Human Rights Campaign is the United States' largest lobbying and policy organization. The religion and faith program creates resources on the relationship between religion and the LGBTQ community and activates faith communities to end discrimination against LGBTQ+ people and ensure equality for all.

National LGBTQ Task Force's Institute for Welcoming Resources

welcomingresources.org

The Task Force, as it's known, trains and mobilizes millions of activists across the United States to ensure "you can be you." The Institute for Welcoming Resources trains communities on faith-based community organizing as well as acts as a hub for resources coming from a variety of religious traditions—all in service to activating people of faith for LGBTQ equality.

Showing Up for Racial Justice

surj.org/our-work/surj-faith

Showing Up for Racial Justice organizes white people for racial and economic justice. The faith arm of the organization works with white people of a variety of faiths with a particular focus on educating and organizing white Christians away from racism and white supremacy.

REALLY COOL SECULAR ADVOCACY ORGANIZATIONS

Several of these were referenced throughout this book. You can use them as resources to focus and enhance your advocacy, even if they don't approach their issues from a faith perspective.

Amnesty International

amnesty.org

Amnesty is a global grassroots movement protecting human rights and responding to the violations of those rights. The organization reports facts and abuses of human rights and tells the stories of people in order to lobby governments toward greater human rights protections for all citizens.

Connections Lab

connectionslab.org

This organization educates advocates on effective messaging and communication. It conducts workshops on framing values and helps build messages about breaking news.

Fair Fight

fairfight.com

There are actually two sides of this organization: Fair Fight and Fair Fight Action. Fair Fight is a nonpartisan 501(c)(3), while Fair Fight Action is a 501(c)(4). Fair Fight got a lot of attention after Stacey Abrams's unsuccessful run for Georgia governor. Both organizations promote fair elections in Georgia and around the country, encourage voter participation in elections, and educate voters about elections and their voting rights.

Human Rights First

humanrightsfirst.org

Human Rights First believes that the United States should be a leader in the movement for human rights around the globe. It advocates to both the government and corporations to respect human rights and the rule of law.

Human Rights Watch

hrw.org

Human Rights Watch is a network of experts, lawyers, and journalists of various countries who investigate and report on human rights abuses. It pushes governments and businesses to change or enforce laws in order to better protect vulnerable people around the globe.

TransLash

translash.org

This transgender-led media organization creates, curates, and presents trans-affirming content, resources, and events in collaboration with trans people and their allies. The outlet employs videos, blog posts, and podcasts to tell the story of transgender people and their lives today.

POLITICAL AND PARTISAN ORGANIZATIONS

Sometimes our advocacy needs to be more partisan. If you are feeling like entering the political realm, try these trusted guides to make strategic choices about donations, volunteer actions, and possibly even running yourself.

DemCast
demcast.com

> DemCast organizes and mobilizes people to effectively use their social media accounts to combat online disinformation. It helps provide accurate information for clarifying the truth and creates calls to action with curated media, graphics, videos, articles, and tool kits.

Democratic Socialists of America (DSA)
dsausa.org

> You have likely heard of the DSA through some of their champions, like Senator Bernie Sanders and Representatives Alexandria Ocasio-Cortez and Rashida Tlaib. It describes itself as a political and activist organization, not a political party. The organization's main objectives are to weaken the power of corporations and increase the power of working people.

Into Act!on Content Library
library.into-action.us

> This library features artwork, graphics, gifs, and memes from a movement of designers, illustrators, animators, and artists. The content is created to be shared on social media and digital platforms, creating an artistic, unified,

and progressive message in response to the issues affecting our country and world.

Movement Briefing: Independent Strategic Research Collaborative

researchcollaborative.org

This hub provides research and messaging resources to help build an equitable and multiracial society. The organization provides movement briefings and messaging guidance to build long-term narratives to compel our country toward democracy.

Oath Advising

oath.vote or oathadvising.com

Oath's founder, Brian Derrick, wants people to make strategic and impactful political donations rather than donating to the candidates who are getting the most attention. Oath produces a free newsletter and Brian posts informative Instagram stories with strategic advice for the most impactful political donations from local to national races. It provides data and recommendations for what donations will achieve your particular goals, whether that is protecting democracy, climate justice, reproductive health, LGBTQ equality, or a variety of other issues.

If you want to go a step further, Oath Advising is the consulting arm. Experts will work with you to create personalized road maps to maximize your impact by identifying candidates pivotal to advancing your individual goals.

Run for Something

runforsomething.net

Think about running for office! Run for Something recruits young progressives to run for office and supports them with a strategic plan and a candidate support system. This helps build the next generation of progressive political leaders.

Swing Left

swingleft.org

Swing Left organizes and directs donations and volunteering efforts to progressive elections and candidates. It does this through a variety of programs. Blueprint is a road map to guide political giving for maximum impact. Vote Forward is a program that writes letters to low-frequency voters encouraging them to vote in upcoming elections. Swing Left also hosts campaign actions like phone banking and door knocking, attempting to make political engagement fun and easy.

Working Families Party

workingfamilies.org

This is an actual political party built from several progressive advocacy organizations with chapters in eighteen states and the District of Columbia. Sometimes it runs candidates on the Democratic Party ticket, and sometimes it does so on its own stand-alone ticket. Its advocacy and its candidates have often had the effect of pulling the Democratic primary in a more progressive direction.

In addition to the sampling of organizations listed above, every state and many localities have organizations that are focused on particular communities or chapters of national organizations. You can also find local organizations that will address climate, housing, education, health care, workers' rights, racial justice, LGBTQ equality, and gender equity.

If your community doesn't have an organization applicable to your advocacy, you always have the option to start one yourself.

FURTHER STUDY: BOOKS AND MORE

Abrams, Stacey. *Minority Leader: How to Lead from the Outside and Make Real Change.* New York: Henry Holt, 2018.

> This is a personal skills development book for people in leadership, especially those who don't come from a place of privilege. Abrams uses her experience and hard-won insights to break down how ambition, fear, money, and failure function in leadership while offering personal stories that illuminate practical strategies.

———. *Our Time Is Now: Power, Purpose, and the Fight for a Fair America.* New York: Henry Holt, 2020.

> Abrams pairs research on history and government with anecdotes from her life and others' who have fought throughout our country's history for the power to be heard. Abrams pairs encouragement with concrete action steps to be an informed and active participant in US democracy. Her book covers steps to ending voter suppression, empowering citizens, and making our government work for the people.

Barber, William J., II. *Revive Us Again: Vision and Action in Moral Organizing.* Boston: Beacon, 2018.

> Rev. Barber joins various contributors to speak to the movements that are leading the fight for security, sustainability,

and prosperity, including Black Lives Matter, the fight for a $15 minimum wage, the struggle to protect voting rights, the march for women's rights, and the movement to overcome poverty and unite the dispossessed across all dividing lines. You will read sermons or addresses from Rev. Barber, followed by the perspectives of the partners he's built coalitions with.

———. *The Third Reconstruction: Moral Mondays, Fusion Politics, and the Rise of a New Justice Movement.* Boston: Beacon, 2016.

This book outlines Rev. Barber's efforts to lay the groundwork for the Moral Mondays movement. These weekly protests outside the North Carolina state capitol blossomed into the largest social movement the South has seen since the civil rights era. He draws on the lessons of history to offer a vision of a new Reconstruction, one in which a diverse coalition of citizens Black and white, religious and secular, northern and southern labors side-by-side for racial and economic justice for all Americans.

———. *We Are Called to Be a Movement.* New York: Workman, 2020.

This book is a printed version of Rev. Barber's sermon calling us to come together and renounce the politics of rejection, division, and greed in favor of the common good and democracy. Like any good sermon, it challenges us and calls us to action.

Duncombe, Stephen, and Steve Lambert. *The Art of Activism: Your All-Purpose Guide to Making the Impossible Possible.* New York: OR Books, 2021.

This book, by the cofounders of the Center for Artistic Activism, combines the creative power of the arts with the strategic planning of activism. It features contemporary and historic stories, cultural and cognitive theory, popular culture, and innovative marketing techniques. It is designed to help people integrate artistry and activism.

Ganz, Marshall.

Ganz created papers, worksheets, and teaching documents focused on the power of storytelling to change minds and compel people into action. He breaks down the types of stories into "story of self," "story of us," and "story of now." Each type of story is different in its audience and impact. The following two resources contain those relevant materials.

———. "Marshall Ganz: The Power of Storytelling." Global Academy Media, November 6, 2017. https://www.globalacademy.media/video/marshall-ganz-power-storytelling/.

This is an interview with Marshall Ganz, who explains how his storytelling model worked for President Obama.

———. "What Is Public Narrative: Self, Us and Now (Public Narrative Worksheet)." Working paper, Kennedy School of Government, 2009. https://dash.harvard.edu/bitstream/handle/1/30760283/Public-Narrative-Worksheet-Fall-2013-.pdf.

This is a worksheet intended to help you focus on your story of self. It is an exercise in leadership that can teach you how to motivate others to join you in action on behalf of a shared purpose.[1]

Ginwright, Shawn. *The Four Pivots: Reimagining Justice, Reimagining Ourselves*. Berkeley: North Atlantic Books, 2022.

Shawn Ginwright, PhD, breaks down the common myths of social movements—sets of deeply ingrained beliefs that actually hold us back from healing and achieving sustainable systemic change. He shows us why our existing frames don't work, proposing instead four revolutionary pivots for better activism and collective leadership. He uses a trauma-informed method to address how we build community. This book shows us how to discover new lenses and boldly assert our need for connection, transformation, trust, wholeness, and healing.

Graves-Fitzsimmons, Guthrie. *Just Faith: Reclaiming Progressive Christianity*. Minneapolis: Broadleaf, 2020.

Graves-Fitzsimmons advocates for progressive Christianity in the public sphere. He lays out the history and present of the progressive Christian movement and the biblical, theological, and cultural Christian grounding for the progressive movement.

Greenberg, Leah, and Ezra Levin. *We Are Indivisible: A Blueprint for Democracy after Trump*. New York: One Signal, 2019.

> Greenberg and Levin share how, following the 2016 election, they circulated a memo helping despondent Americans understand how the US political system works in reality and how citizens could continue to exercise their power. That memo turned into a movement, with Indivisible chapters popping up all over the country and successfully lobbying against the repeal of the Affordable Care Act. This book is an expansion of that memo, coupled with stories of how the strategies were employed over the last several years.

Henderson-Espinoza, Robyn. *Activist Theology*. Minneapolis: Fortress, 2019.

> Henderson-Espinoza combines academia and activism in order to both inspire and edify the progressive activist. They use a personal and artistic approach but keep the conversation centered on theology.

Hong, Cathy Park. *Minor Feelings: An Asian American Reckoning*. New York: One World, 2021.

> Hong fearlessly and provocatively blends memoir, cultural criticism, and history to expose fresh truths about racialized consciousness in America. As the daughter of Korean immigrants, she grew up steeped in shame, suspicion, and melancholy. She would later understand that these "minor feelings" occur when American optimism contradicts your own reality—when you believe the lies you're told about your own racial identity. Minor feelings are not small; they're dissonant—and in their tension, Hong finds the key to the questions that haunt her. She calls on Asian Americans to not be so meek or hide under being "good" or the "model minority."

Kendi, Ibram X. *How to Be an Antiracist*. New York: One World, 2019.

> Kendi takes readers through a widening circle of anti-racist ideas to explain all forms of racism clearly, understand their poisonous consequences, and work to oppose them in our

systems and in ourselves. Kendi combines ethics, history, law, and science with his own personal story of awakening to antiracism.

Lakoff, George. *Don't Think of an Elephant! Know Your Values and Frame the Debate—the Essential Guide for Progressives*. White River Junction, VT: Chelsea Green, 2004.

This is the definitive handbook for understanding how to communicate effectively about key issues facing America today. It is framed through the messaging of the 2004 presidential election. Lakoff has become a leader in messaging and framing during political and cultural debates.

Lewis, Jacqui. *Fierce Love: A Bold Path to Ferocious Courage and Rule-Breaking Kindness That Can Heal the World*. New York: Harmony, 2021.

Fierce Love lays out nine daily practices for breaking through tribalism and engineering the change we seek. From downsizing our emotional baggage to speaking truth to power to fueling our activism with joy, it demonstrates the power of small, morally courageous steps to heal our own lives, our posse, and our larger communities. Sharing stories that trace her personal reckoning with racism as well as the arc of her journey to an inclusive and service-driven faith, Dr. Lewis shows that kindness, compassion, and inclusive thinking are muscles that can be exercised and strengthened.

Menakem, Resmaa. *My Grandmother's Hands: Racialized Trauma and the Pathway to Mending Our Hearts and Bodies*. Las Vegas: Century Recovery, 2017.

Menakem examines the damage and the physical consequences of discrimination from the perspective of body-centered psychology. He argues that until we learn to heal and overcome the generational anguish of white supremacy, we will all continue to bear its scars.

Nelson, James B. *Embodiment: An Approach to Sexuality and Christian Theology*. Minneapolis: Augsburg, 1979.

The bulk of this book builds out a theological case for gay and lesbian inclusion. It is from the 1970s, so it is rather dated (hence the simply "gay and lesbian inclusion"). However, the way it describes a spectrum of reactions to difference can help you understand your target audience.

Neumark, Heidi B. *Sanctuary: Being Christian in the Wake of Trump*. Grand Rapids, MI: Eerdmans, 2020.

Neumark begins each chapter with a quote from Donald Trump that she defies and dismantles with the power of her own stories—anecdotes about offering shelter for queer youth in her city, supporting immigrants and asylum seekers being harassed by immigration officers, and embracing her church's diversity with a Guadalupe celebration, to name a few.

Popović, Srđa, and Matthew Miller. *Blueprint for Revolution: How to Use Rice Pudding, LEGO Men, and Other Nonviolent Techniques to Galvanize Communities, Overthrow Dictators, or Simply Change the World*. New York: Spiegel & Grau, 2015.

This is a secular book written by an internationally known activist who kept hope alive under the weight of a brutal dictator. It employs personal stories of advocacy and support for other movements around the world. It draws on principles from the storytelling narrative we discuss in this book.

Shirky, Clay. *Here Comes Everybody: The Power of Organizing without Organizations*. New York: Penguin, 2009.

I was taught the contents of this book long before I ever read it. I'm likely to cite material from here or talk about how I applied it to my own ministry and how others can do the same. Shirky examines how the communication landscape has changed and allowed people to organize themselves into groups for support, for advocacy, and also for havoc.

Sit, Tyler. *Staying Awake: The Gospel for Changemakers*. Saint Louis: Chalice, 2021.

Rev. Sit has created a practical book for Christian communities that includes several elements, including worksheets, poetry, and cartoons. He focuses on the intersection between the individual and the worshipping community based on his experience leading New City Church in South Minneapolis, close to where George Floyd was murdered.

Voelkel, Rebecca M. M. *Carnal Knowledge of God: Embodied Love and the Movement for Justice*. Minneapolis: Fortress, 2017.

Rev. Voelkel lays out a theological approach to progressive advocacy that includes the *Via Positiva*, asserting and celebrating bodily integrity and empowerment; the *Via Negativa*, acknowledging and analyzing the ways in which vulnerable bodies are colonized; the *Via Creativa*, artistic expressions of social alternatives; and the *Via Transformativa*, grounded in action in what Voelkel calls inaugural eschatology, which anticipates and works toward a different future.

NOTES

INTRODUCTION

1 Isa 61:1–4.

2 Luke 12:13–21.

CHAPTER 1

1 "LGBTQIA+ Studies: A Resource Guide," Library of Congress, accessed September 12, 2022, https://guides.loc.gov/lgbtq-studies/after-stonewall.

2 Barack Obama, "Presidential Proclamation—Establishment of the Stonewall National Monument," National Archives and Records Administration, June 24, 2016, https://obamawhitehouse.archives.gov/the-press-office/2016/06/24/presidential-proclamation-establishment-stonewall-national-monument.

3 "The 'Sip-In' at Julius' Bar in 1966," National Parks Service, August 20, 2019, https://www.nps.gov/articles/julius-bar-1966.htm.

4 Krystyna Blokhina Gilkis, "Obergefell v. Hodges," Legal Information Institute, September 2018, https://www.law.cornell.edu/wex/obergefell_v._hodges.

5 1 Cor 3:6.

6 B. Zemsky and D. Mann, "Building Organizations in a Movement Moment," *Social Policy: Organizing for Social and Economic Justice* 28, no. 3

(2008): 10–12, https://bethzemsky.com/wp-content/uploads/2018/10/Building-organizations-in-a-movement-moment.pdf.

CHAPTER 2

1 Gen 2:18.
2 John 4:29.
3 Conie Borchardt, "Biracial & Rural," Points of Light Music, accessed November 22, 2021, http://www.pointsoflightmusic.net/p/biracial-rural.html.
4 Leah Greenberg and Ezra Levin, *We Are Indivisible: A Blueprint for Democracy after Trump* (New York: One Signal, 2019).
5 Luke 4:18.
6 Vote Forward (website), accessed November 22, 2021, https://votefwd.org/.
7 Jas 2:17.

CHAPTER 3

1 John 3:1–21.

CHAPTER 4

1 Gen 2:18.

CHAPTER 5

1 George Lakoff, *Don't Think of an Elephant! Know Your Values and Frame the Debate—the Essential Guide for Progressives* (White River Junction, VT: Chelsea Green, 2004).
2 M. Sullivan, "Instead of Trump's Propaganda, How about a Nice 'Truth Sandwich'?," *Washington Post*, June 17, 2018, https://www.washingtonpost.com/lifestyle/style/instead-of-trumps-propaganda-how-about-a-nice-truth-sandwich/2018/06/15/80df8c36-70af-11e8-bf86-a2351b5ece99_story.html.

3 "Welcome to the Indivisible Truth Brigade," Indivisible, accessed August 15, 2022, https://indivisible.org/resource/welcome-indivisible -truth-brigade.

4 Acts 17:16.

5 Acts 17:22.

6 Acts 17:32.

7 J. Dao, "Same-Sex Marriage Issue Key to Some G.O.P. Races," *New York Times*, November 4, 2004, https://www.nytimes.com/ 2004/11/04/politics/campaign/samesex-marriage-issue-key-to -some-gop-races.html.

CHAPTER 6

1 GLAAD and *Them*, "Why Queer Activists Should Direct Their Message to the 'Movable Middle,'" *Them*, April 24, 2019, https:// www.them.us/story/movable-middle-glaad.

2 James B. Nelson, *Embodiment: An Approach to Sexuality and Christian Theology* (Minneapolis: Augsburg, 1979).

3 Greenberg and Levin, *We Are Indivisible*.

4 P. Diverlus, "One Year after #BlackoutTuesday, Have White 'Allies' Actually Kept Their Promises?," *Refinery29*, May 24, 2021, https://www.refinery29.com/en-us/2021/02/10271739/black -squares-allyship-life-after-blackout-tuesday.

5 Acts 9:19.

6 Acts 9:20.

CHAPTER 7

1 *Vision and Expectations: Ordained Ministers in the Evangelical Lutheran Church in America* (Chicago: Evangelical Lutheran Church in America, 1990).

2 David Swartling, *Churchwide Assembly Reports and Records: Assembly Minutes* (Chicago: Evangelical Lutheran Church in America, 2009).

3 "About," MOBI, accessed January 16, 2022, https://mobi-nyc .com/aboutus.

4 1 Cor 3:6.

CHAPTER 8

1 Matt 16:13–15.

CHAPTER 9

1 F. Akinnibi and R. Wahid, "Fear of Rampant Crime Is Derailing New York City's Recovery," *Bloomberg*, July 29, 2022, https:// www.bloomberg.com/graphics/2022-is-nyc-safe-crime-stat -reality/.

2 Luke 18:2–8.

3 A. Ohlheiser, "The Religious, Progressive 'Moral Mondays' in North Carolina," *Atlantic*, July 15, 2013, https://www.theatlantic .com/national/archive/2013/07/North-carolina-moral-monday -protests/313301/.

4 D. McClain, "The Rev. William Barber Is Bringing MLK's Poor People's Campaign Back to Life," *Nation*, May 19, 2017, https:// www.thenation.com/article/archive/rev-william-barber-is -bringing-mlks-poor-peoples-campaign-back-to-life/.

5 W. Barber, "Fundamental Principles of the Poor People's Campaign," in *We Are Called to Be a Movement* (New York: Workman, 2020), 90.

6 Ohlheiser, "Religious, Progressive 'Moral Mondays.'"

7 Marielena Hincapié, foreword to Greenberg and Levin, *We Are Indivisible*.

CHAPTER 10

1 N. Lewis, "Scarves Wrapped around the Church," *Concord*, fall 2007, https://www.reconcilingworks.org/wp-content/uploads/2009/05/downloads_concords_Concord_28_3_Fall_2007.pdf.

2 N. Banerjee, "Advocates Hail Lutheran Act on Gay Clergy Members," *New York Times*, August 17, 2007, https://www.nytimes.com/2007/08/17/us/17lutheran.html.

3 The Center for Artistic Activism (website), accessed February 13, 2022, https://c4aa.org/.

4 Stephen Duncombe and Steve Lambert, *The Art of Activism: Your All-Purpose Guide to Making the Impossible Possible* (New York: OR Books, 2021).

5 Duncombe and Lambert, 90.

6 Duncombe and Lambert, 92–93.

7 Diana Budds, "Black Lives Matter, the Brand," Fast Company, July 9, 2018, https://www.fastcompany.com/3062127/black-lives-matter-the-brand.

8 Jeremy Helligar, "How the Clenched Fist Became a Black Power Symbol," *Reader's Digest*, July 21, 2021, https://www.rd.com/article/history-behind-the-clenched-first-and-the-symbol-for-black-power/.

9 Srđa Popović and Matthew Miller, *Blueprint for Revolution: How to Use Rice Pudding, LEGO Men, and Other Nonviolent Techniques to Galvanize Communities, Overthrow Dictators, or Simply Change the World* (New York: Spiegel & Grau, 2015).

CHAPTER 11

1 David Booth, "What Happened Here? Three Observations about Minnesota's Marriage Vote," MinnPost, November 26, 2012, https://www.minnpost.com/community-voices/2012/11/what-happened-here-three-observations-about-minnesotas-marriage-vote/.

2 Lyndsey Layton, "Michelle Rhee, the Education Celebrity Who Rocketed from Obscurity to Oprah," *Washington Post*, January 12, 2013,

https://www.washingtonpost.com/local/education/michelle
-rhee-the-education-celebrity-who-rocketed-from-obscurity-to
-oprah/2013/01/12/eed4e3d8-5a8c-11e2-9fa9-5fbdc9530eb9
_story.html.

3 M. Neergaard, "Taking a Stand against Antigay Bullying," *Huff-Post*, June 1, 2013, https://www.huffpost.com/entry/taking-a
-stand-against-anti-gay-bullying_b_3368922.

4 P. Greene, "Think Florida's Don't Say Gay Bill Is Bad? Tennessee Is Considering One That's Worse," *Forbes*, April 14, 2022, https://www.forbes.com/sites/petergreene/2022/03/16/think-floridas
-dont-say-gay-law-is-bad-tennessee-is-considering-one-thats
-worse/?sh=6f4cb8396f83.

CHAPTER 12

1 Mark 9:30–37.

2 C. Joughin, "Human Rights Campaign Turns the Internet Red for Marriage Equality," Human Rights Campaign, March 26, 2013, https://www.hrc.org/press-releases/human-rights-campaign
-turns-the-internet-red-for-marriage-equality.

3 Mark 9:33.

CHAPTER 14

1 Exod 3–4.

CHAPTER 15

1 Marshall Ganz, "What Is Public Narrative: Self, Us and Now (Public Narrative Worksheet)" (working paper, Kennedy School of Government, 2009), https://dash.harvard.edu/bitstream/
handle/1/30760283/Public-Narrative-Worksheet-Fall-2013-.pdf.

2 Matt 21:28–32.

3 Matt 6:1–8.

CHAPTER 16

1 E. Jones, *The Better World Shopping Guide: Every Dollar Makes a Difference* (Gabriola Island, BC: New Society, 2012); Better World Shopper (website), accessed March 16, 2022, https://betterworldshopper.org/.

2 "Learn More," Accountable for Equality Action, accessed October 8, 2022, https://accountableforequalityaction.org/learn-more/.

3 "The 2022 Corporate Equality Index," Human Rights Campaign, accessed March 12, 2022, https://www.hrc.org/resources/corporate-equality-index.

4 Moral Rating Agency (website), accessed October 8, 2022, https://moralratingagency.org/.

5 Anna Civik, "About Grab Your Wallet," Grab Your Wallet, accessed March 12, 2022, https://grabyourwallet.org/about-us.

6 Jones, *Better World Shopping Guide*, 10, 25.

7 A. M. Wiersch, *Small Business Credit Survey: 2021 Report on Firms Owned by People of Color* (Washington, DC: Federal Reserve System, n.d.), https://www.newyorkfed.org/medialibrary/FedSmallBusiness/files/2021/sbcs-report-on-firms-owned-by-people-of-color.

8 "Community Supported Agriculture," LocalHarvest, accessed March 12, 2022, https://www.localharvest.org/csa.

9 Language is evolving. The term *Latino* is masculine and inherently exclusive. However, there is no universal agreement on gender-neutral alternatives. While I'm using *Latinx* in this book, its use has been largely limited to the United States. Another alternative proposed by some Spanish speakers has been *Latine*. This terminology will depend on the specifics of the wide variety of Spanish-speaking cultures around the world.

APPENDIX

1 Ganz, "Public Narrative."